Everyday Art

for the Classroom Teacher

By
LINDA ARMSTRONG

COPYRIGHT © 2004 Mark Twain Media, Inc.

ISBN 1-58037-272-4

Printing No. CD-1632

Mark Twain Media, Inc., Publishers
Distributed by Carson-Dellosa Publishing Company, Inc.

Table of Contents

Table of Contents (cont.)

Table of Contents (cont.)

Introduction: Everyday Art

With requirements, mandates, and standards filling school days, it is becoming harder and harder to find time for the arts. The short, easy lessons in this book are designed to fit into even the busiest schedule.

When more time is available, these simple activities may be expanded into more sophisticated projects. For example, a butterfly pattern is included to help students create "stained glass" window decorations with tissue and black construction paper. The project, as presented, can be completed in an hour or less. If there is more time, encourage students to research butterflies in the encyclopedia and create original patterns based on the beautiful and varied wings of actual species.

Since budgets for art are often tight, most of the materials recommended for the projects in this book are either recycled or are standard school supplies. When the activities call for unusual items, alternate projects or substitutions are suggested.

The book is arranged by seasons, but the projects may be done in any order. Additional resources are listed at the back of the book. Check an almanac or an online calendar of unusual holidays for other seasonal inspiration. Artists' birthdays, for example, offer opportunities to introduce concepts such as color theory and composition.

Local historic commemorations, community ethnic celebrations, science news, school events, and popular movies are great sources for unique and timely art projects. Examples of such activities are included in the book as starters. Feel free to adapt them to your specific needs.

Many of the projects may be expanded into other subject areas. Tessellations are beautiful, but they are also mathematical patterns. Blank handmade books are fine art, but they are also great for encouraging the development of writing skills. Corn husk dolls and other Native American crafts are ingeniously designed, but they are also historically important. Creating a planet calls for creativity, but it also requires science skills.

The activities vary in the amount of creativity required from student artists. Some projects are very structured. Others are completely open-ended. Many fall somewhere between the extremes. Every group is different. Start with the level of structure that fits your group, and then build flexibility by dropping in other types of projects. Both structure and freedom are important in art.

This is your book. Use it as a starting place. Substitute, adapt, rearrange, and have fun!

Textured Graphite Assignment Book

Explore the textural possibilities of pencil lines while creating a useful assignment book.

Materials for each assignment booklet

- pencil
- one sheet of $8\frac{1}{2}''$ x 11" cover stock or heavy paper
- 4 copies of the reproducible assignment page (printed on both sides) (You may wish to white out the header on the page before copying.)
- long-reach stapler and staples or embroidery needle and heavy thread

Directions

1. Fold the cover stock and assignment pages in half to form a $5\frac{1}{2}''$ by $8\frac{1}{2}''$ booklet.

2. With the fold on the left side, print the word "Assignments" on the cover.

3. Surround the word with a free-hand rectangle.

4. Fill the entire cover surface with graphite textures.

5. Use such techniques as:

   - drawing parallel contour lines around shapes.
   - varying pressure on the pencil to create lights and darks.
   - using single hatching lines angled in different directions to fill adjacent areas in the design.
   - using crosshatching to create interesting dark areas.
   - creating soft effects by smudging.

6. Fasten each booklet, magazine-style, with two staples on the fold or stitch it with an embroidery needle and heavy thread.

Monday, Date: _____

Assignment: _____

Tuesday, Date: _____

Assignment: _____

Wednesday, Date: _____

Assignment: _____

Thursday, Date: _____

Assignment: _____

Friday, Date: _____

Assignment: _____

- -

Monday, Date: _____

Assignment: _____

Tuesday, Date: _____

Assignment: _____

Wednesday, Date: _____

Assignment: _____

Thursday, Date: _____

Assignment: _____

Friday, Date: _____

Assignment: _____

All-About-Me Stash Box

Create a personalized supply box for the closet at home or at school.

Materials for each stash box

- old magazines, catalogs, and junk mail
- a shoebox
- white glue
- scissors
- *optional:* a computer-printed name label

Directions

1. Choose pictures that represent your interests.

2. Cut them out.

3. Arrange the pieces several ways. Don't be afraid to overlap or change them.

4. When you are satisfied with your arrangement, glue the pictures down. Be sure to spread the glue evenly over the back of each piece before placing it.

5. Cover the entire outer surface of the box with pictures (except the bottom). Cover the lid too.

6. Allow the glue to dry. Add a name label to the end of the box so you can locate your supplies quickly.

Variation: Make a dream box. Choose pictures of your dream room, your dream career, and your dream car.

Pencil Container

Create a handy accessory for your study corner.

Materials for each pencil container

- clean, empty can
- colored construction paper cut to fit the can
- crayons
- can opener (electric, if possible)
- felt to cushion the base of the can (optional)
- glue

Directions

1. Seal any rough edges by running the opener around the top edge of the can.

2. Remove paper labels.

3. Outdoors, use the side of a crayon on construction paper to make a rubbing of a rough surface such as cement, asphalt, or a tree trunk.

4. Back in the room, glue the textured paper to the can.

5. Using the base of the can as a pattern, cut out a circle of felt. Glue it on the base.

Extension: Create "leather" cans by using strips of masking tape on the cans instead of the textured paper. Apply short strips, laying them on in different directions. Rub on brown shoe polish to color the tape and bring out its "leathery" detail.

Wet-on-Wet Book Covers

Create unique covers for textbooks while exploring wet-on-wet watercolors.

Materials for each book cover

- brown paper grocery sack
- set of watercolor pans
- watercolor brush
- one or two plastic dishpans half-filled with plain water
- newspaper or other work area protection
- scissors
- cellophane tape

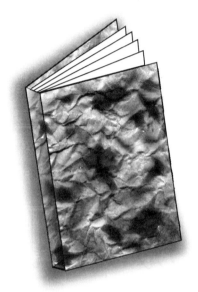

Directions

1. Spread newspaper to protect the tables.

2. Use the brush to drip water on each pan of watercolor to soften.

3. Cut the bottom off the sack.

4. Wad up the brown sack paper to form deep random creases.

5. Open the paper and wet it in the dishpan. Squeeze it very gently to remove excess water. Lay the paper flat on the newspaper-covered table.

6. Dip the brush in one color. The brush should not be too wet. Brush it across the wet, textured paper sack. The pigment will accumulate in the creases.

7. Repeat with other colors. Start with lighter colors and end with black.

8. Let the paper dry completely.

9. Cut and fold the decorated paper to fit your textbook.

A Self-Portrait Still Life

Use three favorite colors and three objects to create a still life that tells a story.

Materials for each crayon painting

- book, filmstrip, or video with reproductions of classic still-life studies (optional)
- paper
- pencils
- crayons
- three small personal items from home, from the classroom, from your desk, or from your pocket

Directions

1. Select three small items. They should all fit on your desk, with enough room left for the drawing paper. Paperback books, personal keys, lunch tickets, game pieces, and combs are possibilities.

2. Study the reproductions, if available, and notice what items the artists used for their still-life paintings. How are your items the same or different?

3. Arrange your items on the desk. Putting a sheet of white paper under them will make shadows easier to see.

4. Sketch your arrangement lightly in pencil. Your drawing should fill the page.

5. Use just three favorite colors. Press down hard on the crayon to create a bright, rich surface.

Easier variation: Trace the three small items over and over to fill your page. Let the tracings overlap. Color the design.

A challenging variation: Do a detailed pencil sketch of your favorite item at home. It could be your computer, your TV, your bed, the refrigerator, your bike, or the basketball hoop in your yard.

Fallen Leaves

Watch leaf shapes emerge like magic as you create these seasonal crayon rubbings.

Materials for each rubbing picture

- one flat, fallen leaf with a distinctive shape and veining
- used crayons without paper sleeves
- standard office copy paper or newsprint

Directions

1. Put your leaf on the table with the vein structure facing up and place a sheet of paper over it.

2. Use a crayon on its side to rub over the paper, revealing the leaf shape.

3. Move the paper and repeat with a different color to create a second textured leaf.

4. Continue until the entire page is covered with overlapping leaf rubbings in various colors.

Create a Color Wheel

Create a color wheel showing the primary and secondary colors.

Materials for each color wheel

- one sheet of $8\frac{1}{2}''$ x 11″ watercolor paper or other paper that will not buckle when wet
- set of watercolors
- brush
- pencil
- color wheel pattern (next page)
- one sheet of carbon paper (may be reused several times)

Directions

1. Use the carbon paper to transfer the pattern to the heavy paper. (Alternate: Use a pencil to cover the back of the pattern paper with graphite, then lay it down on the heavy white paper and go over each line.)

2. Paint the correct color in each circle. (The order of the colors is important.)

Adaptation: If you don't have watercolors, use crayons, markers, or cut the colored circles out of construction paper. Construction paper color wheels are especially dramatic on black backgrounds.

Extension: Try mixing your own green with yellow and blue instead of using the one that is already mixed. What other colors can you mix yourself?

Color Wheel Pattern

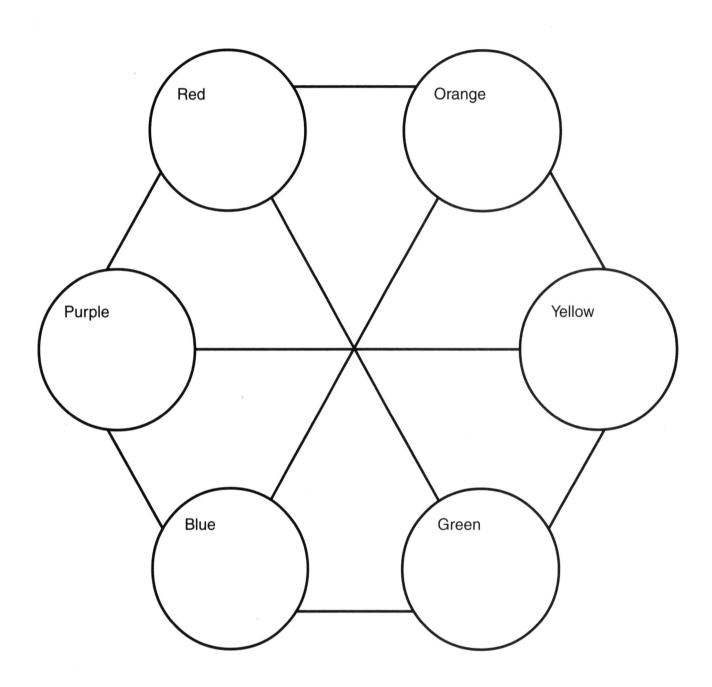

Related Color Scribble: A Work Folder Cover

Use related colors to create a work sample folder for Parents' Night.

Materials for each folder

- one 12" x 18" sheet of folder-weight drawing paper
- crayons

Directions

1. Fold the paper in half to make a folder.

2. Scribble in pencil, creating large intersecting loops that cover the entire front of the folder.

3. Use any three colors that appear side-by-side on the color wheel. (See Color Wheel activity.) Examples include red, orange, and yellow. These are called "related" or "analogous" colors.

5. Color in the areas formed by the pencil scribbles. Try not to repeat the same color in any two adjoining sections.

Extensions:

1. Outline the color areas with black crayon after coloring, or go over the pencil lines with black watercolor marker before coloring.

2. Do the same project on white paper with colored pencils. Notice how the choice of medium alters the effect.

Weaving a Rainy Day Placemat

Make a placemat for those special rainy day lunches at your desk.

Materials for each placemat

- one sheet each, 9″ x 12″ orange and blue construction paper
- scissors
- ruler
- pencil
- glue
- *optional:* clear, self-adhesive shelf paper

Directions

1. Measure off one-inch intervals on the short edges of the orange paper and the long edges of the blue paper.

2. Use the ruler to draw lines between the marks.

3. Cut the blue paper into strips along the lines.

4. Measure one inch from the short edges of the orange paper. Use the ruler to draw a line on either side.

5. Fold the orange paper in half, matching short edges, with the lines on the outside.

6. Starting at the folded edge, cut along each line. Do not cut past the one-inch limit.

7. Weave the blue strips in and out of the orange paper, creating a checkerboard pattern.

8. Glue all of the ends down on both sides.

Variation: Use related colors instead of complementary colors: orange and red or orange and yellow.

Optional: Cover your placemat with clear, self-adhesive shelf paper to make it waterproof.

Making Posters

Whether they are for a school carnival, a class election, or the last yard sale of the season, good signs and posters spell success.

Materials for each poster

- white tagboard or poster board
- markers: black and bright colors

Directions

1. Look at examples of effective signs.
   - The letters are large and simple.
   - Words are easy to see because of high-contrast color schemes.
   - The letters themselves convey a tone or message.
   - Illustrations are simple.
   - Spelling and grammar are correct.

2. Choose a subject for your poster. Simplify your message to one or two words.

3. Use a ruler and a pencil to draw guidelines. These lines will keep your words straight.

4. Draw the letters in pencil before you color them with marker.

Hints: Since the poster is white, dark colors will be the easiest to read. If you want to use red or green, outline the letters in black after you finish. It will make them stand out.

13

Class Election Tags

Show your true colors. Convince everyone to support your candidate.

Materials for four campaign tags

- one sheet of $8\frac{1}{2}''$ x 11" construction paper
- tag patterns (on the next page)
- markers
- scissors
- catalogs, magazines, and junk mail
- glue
- a paper punch and string or 4 safety pins

Directions

1. Use the patterns on the next page to cut out four tags from the construction paper.

2. Print your message in pencil, and then go over the letters with marker.

3. Decorate your campaign tags with drawings, computer graphics, or magazine pictures.

4. Create a button hanger by punching a hole through the top of the tag and running a string through it, or fasten the paper to your shirt with a safety pin.

Extension: Study the advertisements used in a national or state election. How do the candidates use pictures to convey ideas?

Campaign Tag Patterns

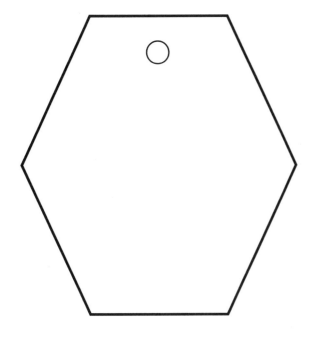

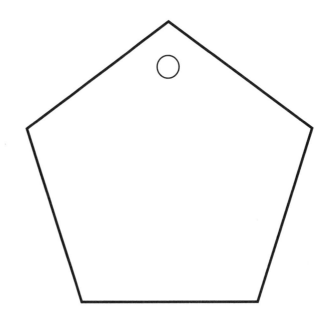

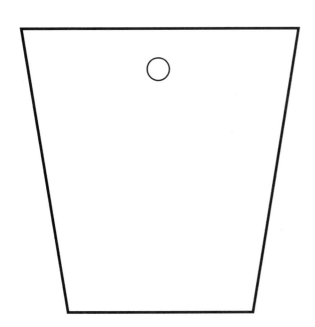

15

Design a School Flag

Every nation has a flag. Every state has a flag. Even cities and organizations have flags. Design a flag for your school.

Materials for each design

- one large sheet of newsprint and one 8½″ x 11″ sheet of white paper
- pencil
- ruler
- crayons or markers
- *optional:* pictures of flags from an almanac, encyclopedia, illustrated dictionary, or the Internet

Directions

1. Fold the newsprint into eighths.

2. Draw a rectangle in each eighth.

3. Think about what makes your school different from other schools. How could you show those special qualities in symbols?

4. Sketch at least eight possible flags. Use stripes, stars, and other simple symbols.

5. Choose your best sketch and draw it on the white copy paper.

6. Color your flag with crayons or markers.

"Workers on Campus" Photo Shoot

Celebrate Labor Day by honoring the men and women who work at your school.

Materials for the class

- one 27-exposure disposable camera
- processing with double prints
- an adult assistant to accompany student photographers to appointments

Directions

For each student photographer:

1. List all of the adults who work at the school.

2. Choose someone from the list to photograph.

3. At least a week in advance, write your subject a letter explaining the project. Request an appointment to take the photograph.

4. Pose your subject outdoors in front of a plain wall.

5. The sun should be shining over your shoulder. It should be lighting up your subject's face. Don't let clouds stop you. Bright, cloudy days are terrific for taking pictures of people.

6. Look through the viewfinder (the little window on the camera). Move in closer until you see your subject from the waist up.

7. Press the button to take just one picture.

8. Thank your subject.

9. When everyone in your class has had a turn and the pictures have been processed, create a bulletin board display with the photos.

10. Write a letter to your subject thanking him or her for all the work he or she does at the school. Enclose the extra print.

Alternate: Use school pictures to draw 8½″ x 11″ portraits of staff members.

Seasonal Reflection

Autumn woods are doubly beautiful when reflected in a lake. An old tempera trick makes this fall classic easy.

Materials for each painting

- one sheet of painting paper
- liquid tempera in the following colors: blue, red, yellow, orange, brown, and green
- a brush
- a container of water
- *optional:* photographs of trees or a walk outside to look at tree trunks and branches

Directions

1. Fold the paper in half, matching long sides, and then unfold it.

2. Dip your brush in water, then in blue paint. Using more water than color, paint the top half of the paper blue. Using the same technique, paint the bottom half of the paper green.

3. Let the thin paint dry completely.

4. Using short brush strokes and thick paint, paint red, yellow, and orange trees just above the fold line. Work quickly. Fold the paper over while the paint is still wet. Press it down evenly, then lift it up. You will have reflections in your green lake.

5. Let the trees dry. Dip the wooden end of your brush into the brown paint. Add trunks and branches to the trees above the fold. A trunk is similar to a capital Y, but not as symmetrical. One of the separating branches is usually larger than the other.

Tissue Paper Collage

Autumn is a season of warm colors. Use them to create a cozy collage.

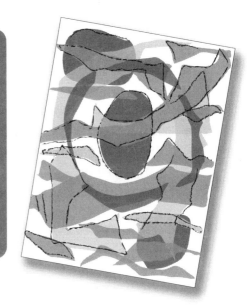

Materials for each collage

- one sheet of heavy white paper that will not buckle, 9″ x 12″
- one half-sheet each, red, yellow, and orange tissue paper
- liquid starch in a cup or milk carton
- water in a cup or milk carton
- tempera paintbrush
- *optional:* black marker

Directions

1. Tear random shapes out of the tissue paper.

2. Place one of the tissue pieces on the white paper.

3. Dip the brush in starch, and then wipe the excess off on the rim of the cup.

4. Paint the starch over the tissue to adhere it, but do not go beyond the edges.

5. Place another tissue piece so it overlaps part of the first. Paint over it in the same way. Notice what happens where the two overlap.

6. Repeat until most of the paper is covered with tissue.

Extension: After the starch dries, trace around the edge of each shape formed by the overlapping tissues with black watercolor marker.

Watercolor Glazes: Leaf Shapes

Have you ever seen leaves in a stream in autumn? This painting may remind you of those bright layers of color.

Materials for each painting

- watercolor paper or other paper that will not buckle when wet
- watercolors: red, yellow, and orange
- autumn leaf or the maple leaf pattern on the next page
- watercolor brush
- container of water

Directions

1. Place the leaf pattern on the watercolor paper. Trace around it, and then move it to another spot and trace it again. Trace it a total of three times.

2. Paint the whole paper yellow, except the leaf shapes. Allow the paint to dry.

3. Trace the pattern again in a different spot. It will overlap parts of the previous leaf shapes, which are still white, and parts of the yellow areas. Trace the leaf pattern a total of three more times.

4. Paint everything orange except the leaf shapes you just traced. You will paint over some white areas and some yellow areas. Watch what happens when you paint over the yellow. Does it remind you of the tissue paper collage?

5. Allow the paint to dry.

6. Trace the leaf or the pattern three more times.

7. Use the red watercolor next. Paint everything except your most recent leaf shapes. This may be confusing. Do the best you can. It will look great even if you make a few mistakes. Advanced groups may add more layers.

Maple Leaf Pattern

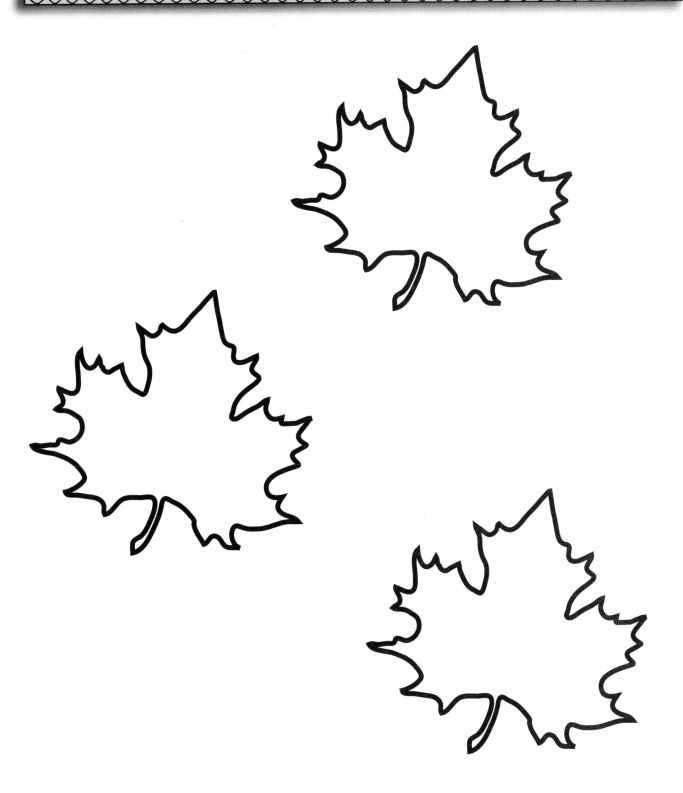

Crayon Scrafito: Smoke and Fire

On cool autumn nights, some people gather around campfires to sing and tell stories. Create a glowing evening scene with crayon.

Materials for one scratch painting

- 9" x 12" light cardboard
- crayons in warm colors, plus black
- an unbent paper clip, or a nail
- cover the tables with newspapers

Directions

1. Color random areas of the cardboard red, yellow, orange, and other warm colors. Press hard and fill the entire surface of the cardboard with crayon.

2. Cover the red, orange, and yellow with black crayon. Color the entire page. Do not let any color show through.

3. Use the sharp end of the paper clip to reveal the colors underneath. Scratch out a campfire scene.

Apple Banner: An Alternating Pattern

John Chapman, better known as Johnny Appleseed, was born on September 26, 1775. Celebrate the event with this apple design.

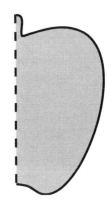

Materials for one section of the pattern

- white paper 8″ x 8″
- red construction paper 8″ x 8″
- scissors
- pencil
- apple pattern
- glue or paste

Directions

1. Fold the red paper in half once in each direction to create four 4″ squares.

2. Unfold and cut the squares apart along the fold lines.

3. Fold one of the 4″ squares in half. Starting at the fold, cut half an apple shape.

4. Keep both pieces, the apple and the square with the apple-shaped hole.

5. Paste the square with the apple-shaped hole in the top left corner of the white paper, matching the top and the left side.

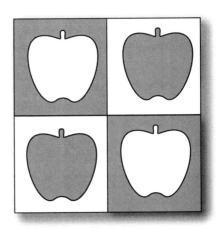

6. Paste the apple in the center of the white square, so that, on the top row, you have a red square with a white apple and a white square with a red apple.

7. Repeat steps 3 and 4 with a second small square. Paste the second red square with the apple-shaped hole in the lower right corner, matching the side and bottom.

8. Paste the red apple in the center of the white square.

Extension: Put all of the apple pattern sections together to form a banner, a bulletin board, or a frieze above the chalkboard.

Make a Papier-Mâché Harvest Bowl

Make a harvest bowl for the kitchen table, so fresh seasonal fruit will always be ready for snacks.

Materials for each bowl

- one ceramic or smooth plastic bowl with sloping sides
- petroleum jelly
- newspapers torn into uneven strips about 1″ x 4″
- wallpaper paste or equivalent
- assorted tempera or acrylic paints, including white

Directions

1. Turn the bowl upside-down and cover the outside evenly with petroleum jelly.

2. Dip each strip of newspaper into the wallpaper paste and lay it on the bowl. Build up several layers.

3. Let it dry.

4. Lift the papier-mâché bowl off of the form.

5. Use tempera or acrylic to paint it white. Let the paint dry.

6. Paint grapes, an apple, or an orange inside. Use the apple pattern from page 23 activity, if desired. Add a stem and one green leaf.

Extension: Use a plain, plastic full-face mask from a costume shop as a form to create a papier-mâché mask. Follow the steps above. Before painting, cut out eye holes.

Mini Still Life: Half an Apple

Look at this apple from many angles.

Materials for each mini still life

- ½ apple
- pencil
- two sheets white copy paper

Directions

1. Pose your apple half on one of the sheets of paper.

2. Draw the apple as you see it.

3. Include the shadows on the white paper.

4. Move the apple half so you have a different view, and then draw the new angle on the same page.

5. Draw the apple at least three times from different angles.

Extension: Draw other seasonal fruits or vegetables.

Cardboard Prints

Make a repeated design with two cardboard printing blocks.

Materials for one page of prints

- corrugated cardboard cut into four 3" squares
- one 9" x 12" sheet of white paper
- thick tempera in two colors
- two foam meat trays or sheets of waxed paper
- two paper towels   •   folded sheet of newspaper
- scissors   •   glue

Cardboard printing blocks

Directions

1. Cut a simple design, such as a diamond or a half-moon, out of one cardboard square. Glue it to the second square.

2. Cut a different design from one of the remaining squares and glue it onto the last square. Let the glue dry.

3. Measure off a 3" x 3" grid on the white paper. Each square will be three inches across.

4. Fold the paper towels and put them in the meat trays or on the waxed paper.

5. Saturate each paper towel with a smooth layer of paint.

6. Press the first block into one color, and then print it in the first square.

7. Press the other block into the second color, and then print it in the second square.

8. Continue to alternate, filling each square with a print.

Extension: Find alternating designs on textiles, wall coverings, wrapping paper, or other products.

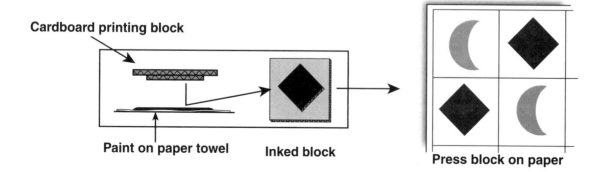

Cardboard printing block

Paint on paper towel   Inked block

Press block on paper

A Tessellation Frame

Make a frame for an autumn drawing.

Materials for one frame

- frame pattern from next page
- brown and orange crayons
- pencil
- ruler

Directions

1. Use a pencil and ruler to complete the design.

2. Color the alternate triangles brown and orange.

3. Draw a picture to fit the frame.

Tesselation Frame Pattern

Blue Pumpkin, Orange Sky

Contemporary painter Jasper Johns painted a flag using complementary colors. His flag is green, black, and orange. If you stare at it and then close your eyes, you will see red, white, and blue. Use his idea to create this variation on a seasonal favorite.

Materials for one pumpkin picture

- one 9" x 12" sheet each of orange and blue construction paper
- one small piece of red construction paper for the stem
- scissors
- paste or glue
- pumpkin pattern from next page
- pencil

Directions

1. Cut out and then trace the pumpkin pattern onto the blue paper.

2. Cut out the blue pumpkin shape.

3. Cut along the dotted lines.

4. Place the pieces slightly apart. Let a little orange paper show between the sections.

5. Glue the sections down on the orange paper.

6. Cut out and trace the stem pattern onto the red paper.

7. Cut the stem out and glue it on the orange paper.

8. Stare at your blue pumpkin for one minute, and then close your eyes.

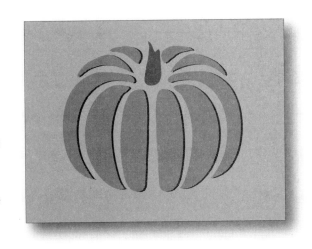

Pumpkin Pattern

Fold

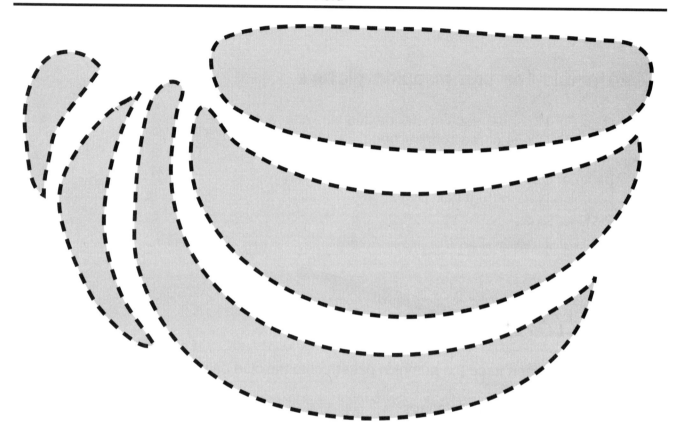

Stem

Queen Elizabeth I's Birthday: Design a Crown

Queen Elizabeth I, one of England's greatest monarchs, was born on September 7, 1533. Celebrate her birthday by designing a royal crown.

Materials for one crown

- strip of white heavy paper 4-5″ wide and 24″ long
- small pieces of aluminum foil, paper-backed foil wrapping paper, or colored construction paper for "jewels"
- *optional:* sequins or glitter glue
- scissors
- glue
- staples
- pencil
- markers
- *optional:* pictures of authentic royal crowns from the library, encyclopedia, or Internet

Directions

1. Study pictures of real crowns, if possible.

2. Mark the center of the paper strip. It will sit at the center of your forehead.

3. Draw the basic shape of your crown. It is a hat; it should be symmetrical. Cut it out. (Do not cut off any of the paper's length. Cut the shape from the width only.)

4. Cut jewel shapes from the colored paper and foil. Glue them onto the crown. Add facets with markers.

5. Staple the ends of the crown together to form a ring that fits your head. Trim off the extra paper.

Extension: If the crown were part of a costume for a play, what else would you need?

Charcoal Drawings on Newspaper

The first daily newspaper in the United States was published on September 21, 1784. To celebrate, recycle old news into art.

Materials

- classified ad section of the newspaper
- sticks of medium to soft artist's charcoal
- still life including seasonal vegetables
- *optional*: white artist's pastel
- *optional*: clamp-on hardware lights with aluminum reflectors

*Note: if possible, set up four simple still lifes, one on each side of the room, so everyone can see easily.

Directions

1. Use charcoal to draw the still life.

2. Observe carefully.

3. Do not draw lines. Color in all of the shadows you see.

4. Notice how shadows define the light areas of the picture.

5. Notice how the lines of print become simple texture.

Extension: Use the classifieds to practice portrait drawing. Choose a partner. Draw that person, and then take your turn posing.

Action Lines

Use action sports photographs to help you learn to draw figures.

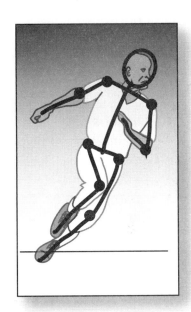

Materials for each action line study

- one newspaper sports section with photographs
- pencil or fine-line markers
- scissors
- white copy paper
- paste or glue

Directions

1. Cut out 2 action photographs.

2. Paste the pictures to the paper.

3. With the pencil or marker, draw a stick person inside each figure in the photo showing the action.

4. Mark elbows and knees with small circles.

5. Don't forget the shoulders and hips.

6. Draw the same stick figures in blank sections of the white paper.

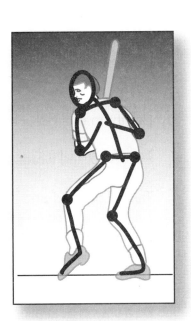

Extensions:
- Draw a figure from one of the pictures.
- Draw stick figures of people sitting, walking, running, and jumping.
- Keep a sketchbook, drawing people as stick figures.
- Look up the work of contemporary painter Keith Haring online.

Headline Paintings

Words from newspapers and magazines can provide inspiration for paintings on days when you run out of ideas.

Materials

- sections of the newspaper with large-print words or bold, colored type
- scissors
- paste or glue
- resealable plastic sandwich bags
- crayons
- drawing paper

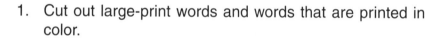

Directions

1. Cut out large-print words and words that are printed in color.

2. Put them in a pile.

3. Pool all of the words in your class. Mix them up.

4. Take a handful and put them in your bag.

5. Pull out three words. Use all three words in a sentence about something. Write the sentence at the bottom of your paper.

6. Do a crayon illustration to go with your sentence.

Extension: Write and illustrate a story that includes your sentence. Bind it into a book.

Tintoretto's Paradise

The painter Jacopo Robusti, known as Tintoretto, was born on September 16, 1518. He did a huge, complex painting called "Paradise." Paradise is a perfect place. What is your idea of a perfect place?

Materials for one picture of the perfect place:

- magazines, catalogs, used greeting cards, and junk mail with pictures
- scissors
- glue
- black fine-line marker
- colored markers
- scraps of colored paper
- white drawing paper

Directions

1. Think about what the word "perfect" means to you.

2. Choose items from the magazines that would fit in your perfect world.

3. Glue them to the white drawing paper.

4. Add more details with markers and shapes cut from the colored paper.

Equinox Symmetry

On September 22, day and night are twelve hours each. This only happens twice a year. Celebrate the symmetry with this paper-cutting project.

Materials for each symmetrical picture

- 9" x 12" sheet of white construction paper
- 4" x 6" sheet of black construction paper
- scissors
- pencil
- glue or paste
- patterns

Directions

1. Trace one of the patterns on each side of the black sheet.

2. Cut out each shape.

3. Reverse the cut piece and place it directly across from the cut space as a mirror image.

4. Glue the large black shape down in the center of the white paper.

5. Glue the reversed shapes in place.

Easier: Use a large sheet of white drawing paper and a 9" x 12" sheet of black paper. Lay the lower edge of your palm against the short edge of the black paper. Trace around your hand, and then cut out the tracing. Flip the cut-out over. Paste both pieces on the white paper, forming mirror-image black and white hands.

Equinox Symmetry Patterns

Columbus Day: Create a Compass Rose

When Christopher Columbus sailed west for India, he carried maps and charts. Each map had a symbol called a compass rose, a pair of four-pointed stars, one on top of the other. Each star point indicated a compass direction. Now, as in the days of Columbus, mapmakers make these beautiful as well as informative designs. Create your own compass rose.

Materials

- white paper
- pencil
- ruler
- colored pencils or fine-line color markers
- compass rose pattern from the next page

Directions

1. Start with the pattern.

2. Draw a four-pointed star using the longer lines as guides.

3. Label the points N, S, E, and W.

4. Add a point between each main point (the shorter lines). Label these new points NE, SE, SW, and NW. This is called a compass rose.

5. Decorate your compass rose. Make it as colorful as you wish.

Extension: Many sailors in the days of Columbus believed in sea monsters. Draw a different sea monster for each of the four directions. Get ideas for your monsters from pictures of prehistoric sea creatures or such denizens of the deep as the giant squid.

Compass Rose Pattern

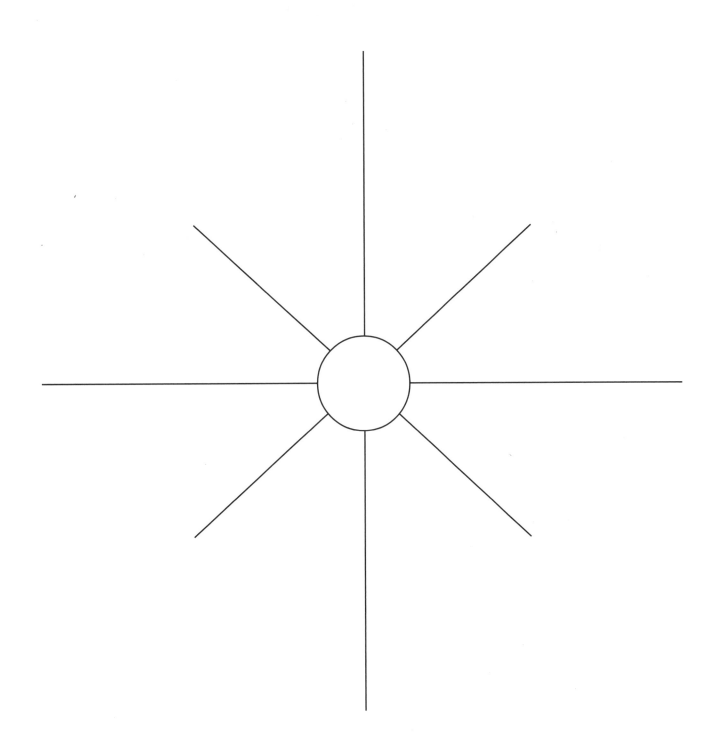

An Illuminated Word

Celebrate Children's Book Week by revisiting a time before the invention of the printing press, when all books were created by hand.

Materials

- paper
- fine-line colored markers or colored pencils
- ruler
- pencil
- eraser
- handwriting book

Directions

1. Choose your favorite word.

2. Use the ruler to draw guidelines. The letters in the main part of your word will be one inch high.

3. At the beginning of your word, draw a square two inches wide and two inches high.

4. Pressing very lightly with your pencil, print the letter that begins your word as a capital. It should fill the box.

5. Sketch decorations around the capital letter that fit the meaning of your word. For example, the "R" in rain could be surrounded by raindrops, puddles, and umbrellas.

6. Using your pencil and the guidelines in a handwriting book, print the rest of the letters.

7. Go over all of the letters with a fine-line black marker.

8. Color the pictures around the capital letter with colored marker or colored pencil.

Extension: Print out a font from a computer word-processing program. Copy it or use it as a starting point for creating your own letter set.

Favorite Character Pop-up Puppets

Is your favorite book character a student wizard? A writing spider? A white rabbit? Create a character stick puppet with its own stage.

Materials for each puppet

- small white cup
- craft stick
- 1″ Styrofoam™ ball
- 5″ square of lightweight cloth (choose the best from several colors)
- circle pattern with 5″ diameter to fit the cloth
- rubber band or a piece of string
- fine-line colored markers
- bits of yarn, beads, and other small items
- glue

Directions

1. Choose a piece of cloth that matches your character. For example, Wilbur, the pig, would be pink.

2. Trace the circle onto the cloth and cut it out.

3. Dip the end of the craft stick into glue and then push it into the Styrofoam ball so it is firmly attached. It will be your puppet's head.

4. Put the cloth circle over the ball.

5. Form the neck and hold the loose "body" in place by looping the rubber band tightly around the cloth and the stick just under the ball.

6. Push the craft stick through the bottom of the cup. You will be able to raise and lower your puppet.

7. Use markers, beads, yarn, and colored paper to add features.

8. Color the cup to create an appropriate "stage." For example, Wilbur's cup would be a pig pen.

Picasso's Birthday: Drawing All the Angles

Pablo Picasso was born on October 25,1881. He helped to develop a kind of painting called "cubism." A cubist painting is like a sculpture. It shows all sides of the subject at once.

Materials for one "cubist" painting

- crayons in black, brown, red, and orange
- pencil
- drawing paper
- student model
- three sheets of blank newsprint

Directions

1. On the newsprint, draw the model's head and shoulders from the front, from the side, and from the back.

2. Combine all of the drawings into a head and shoulders view that includes parts of each drawing. Your picture will not look like the model! One eye might be seen straight on, while the nose might be viewed from the side.

3. Use brown, red, and orange to color the picture. Add details with black.

Extension:

- Look up Picasso in the encyclopedia. Study some of his portraits. Look for details from many angles.

- Set up a simple still life on your desk. It should have two or three items. Sketch it from several angles, and then use parts of each of the sketches to create a new drawing.

Hokusai's Birthday: A Different Perspective

The Japanese master of printmaking, Hokusai, was born in October. He created dramatic illusions of distance without using European perspective techniques. Practice making trees look close or far away.

Materials

- three sheets of colored construction paper in dark brown, dark tan, and blue-gray or pale blue
- scissors
- white paper
- glue or paste
- tree patterns from the next page

Directions

1. Trace the pattern of the large tree on the dark brown paper and cut it out.

2. Trace the pattern of the medium-sized tree on the dark tan paper and cut it out.

3. Trace the pattern of the small tree on the blue-gray or pale blue paper and cut it out.

4. Arrange the trees on the page in different ways. See which arrangement creates the greatest illusion of depth.

Hints from Hokusai:

✤ Objects lower on the page seem nearer. Objects higher on the page seem farther away.

✤ Large objects seem nearer. Smaller objects seem farther away.

✤ An object that is in front of another object is closer.

✤ Darker objects seem closer than objects that are colored in middle tones.

✤ Detailed objects seem nearer than objects with less detail.

✤ Warm colors seem closer than cool colors.

Tree Patterns

Harvest Moon: Crayon Resist

Recreate a magical autumn evening with crayon and black watercolor or thin tempera.

Materials for one painting

- paper for painting
- crayons (light colors and white)
- black watercolor or thin black tempera paint
- water container
- paintbrush

Directions

1. Draw an autumn night scene with crayons in pale colors. Press down hard to deposit a lot of wax. Possible things to draw:

    - a bonfire or campfire
    - a full moon
    - stars
    - clouds
    - wet streets with reflections
    - city lights and lighted signs
    - the front of a movie theater or cafe

2. Paint over the entire page with black paint and watch your drawing glow.

Grocery Sack Kachina Masks

Native Americans lived on the North American continent long before European explorers arrived. During ceremonies, dancers from the Pueblo tribes of the Southwest wore masks to represent powerful forces in their lives. Design your own mask to represent friendship, athletic ability, or another quality important to you.

Materials for one mask

- large, brown paper grocery sack
- scissors
- colored paper (assorted colors)
- glue
- markers

Directions

1. Put the sack over your head and mark the location of your eyes. Cut holes so you can see.

2. Cut features and hair out of colored paper. Glue them on. Study pictures of Kachina masks for ideas.

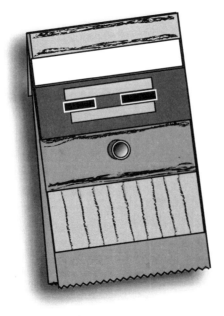

Paper Plate Masks

Sometimes, Native American masks represented animals. Use a paper plate to help you become your favorite animal.

Materials for one mask

- paper plate
- scissors
- markers
- colored paper
- glue
- narrow elastic or narrow ribbon
- stapler and staples

Directions

1. Cut a triangle out of the bottom of the plate so it fits over your nose.

2. Cut holes in the plate for your eyes.

3. Use the markers and colored paper to add ears, whiskers, manes, and other distinctive animal details.

4. Cut the elastic long enough to reach around your head, or cut two pieces of ribbon long enough to tie. Staple the ends of the elastic or the ribbon ties to the back of the mask.

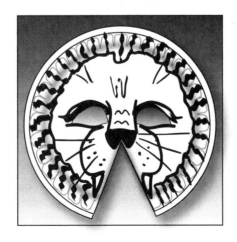

Corn Husk Dolls

Native American children taught the children of European settlers how to make dolls out of corn husks. You can make them too.

Materials for one doll

- nine corn husks (available in the Latino foods section of the supermarket)
- rubber bands or string
- markers
- glue
- *optional:* fabric scraps

Directions

1.   Soften the husks by soaking them in water.

2.   Fasten four husks together at the top with a rubber band.

3.   The banded top will be inside the doll's head. Hold the top upside-down and turn each husk down in a different direction around the top as if you were peeling a banana.

4.   Put another rubber band around the "neck."

5.   Roll the fifth softened husk. Slip it under one of the four husks that are hanging down below the doll's neck. The rolled one will stick out on either side to form the doll's arms. Put another rubber band around the body just below the arms.

6.   Put a rubber band near the end of each arm to form the wrists.

7.   With another rubber band, attach four more husks to the waist of the doll. Leave them loose to form a skirt, or separate them into two legs for pants. Cover these rubber bands with strips of husk.

8.   Let the doll dry, and then decorate it with markers and dress it with scraps of fabric.

Alternate: Use softened strips of husks to tie parts of the doll in place instead of rubber bands.

Native American Beadwork Design

Native Americans used beautiful geometric designs on their pots, jewelry, rugs, blankets, and baskets. Design a repeating beadwork pattern.

Materials:

- graph paper from the next page
- colored pencils or markers
- pencil

Directions

1. Design a beadwork square on the graph paper. Look at the examples below for ideas.

2. Repeat your square. Every detail, including the colors, should be repeated.

Examples:

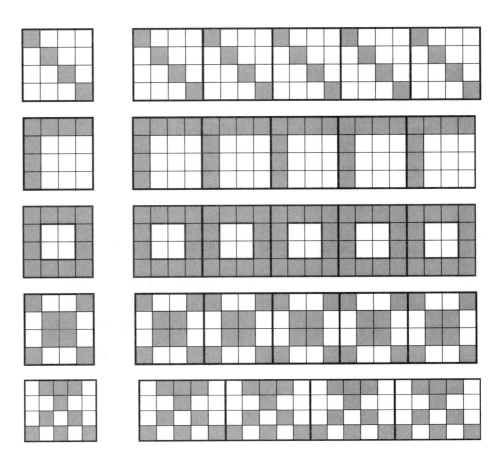

Graph Paper for Beadwork Design

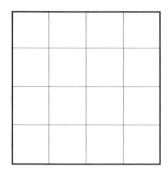

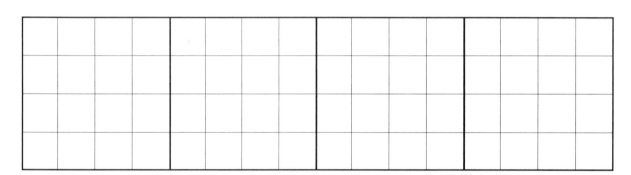

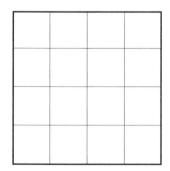

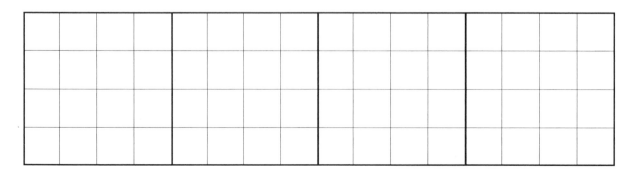

50

Four Directions

Southwest tribes make paintings of colored sand. The paintings use the four directions, north, south, east, and west. They repeat a design once in each direction to create a four-way repeating design.

Materials:

- graph paper from the next page
- colored pencils or markers

Directions

1. Start in one corner of the top left square of the graph paper. Make a mark in one color.

2. Repeat the mark on the opposite side of the opposite square to create a mirror image. Create a mirror image of the top two squares in the bottom two squares.

3. Add squares and colors to the design, one square or group at a time, filling in the mirror images as you go.

Extension: Real sand paintings are slightly different for each direction. Find out why.

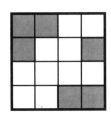

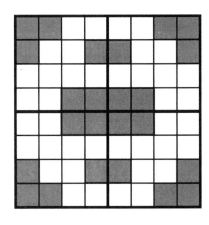

Graph Paper for Sand Painting Designs

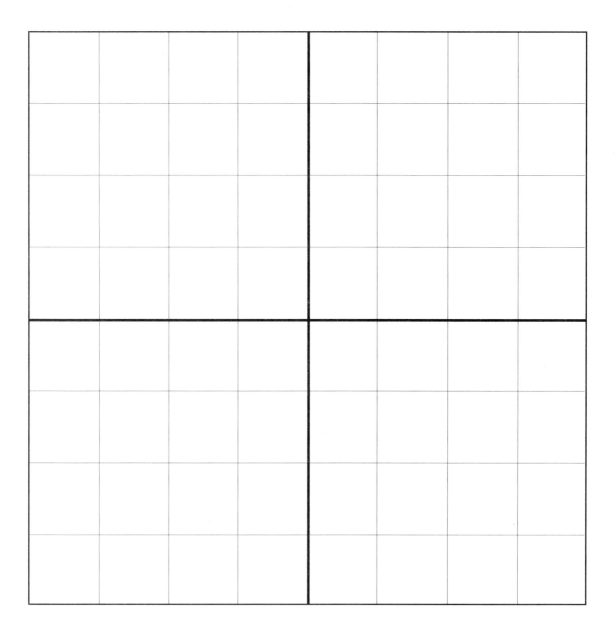

Extension: Transfer your design to sandpaper and color lightly with crayons.

To discuss: Many artists try to create work that will be around long after they die. Some artists, like Native American sand painters, create works that will last only a short time. What is the advantage of each type of art? Name other types of temporary art.

Cardboard Tube Totem Poles

Native Americans who lived in the Pacific Northwest built special towers called "totem poles" to celebrate their ancestors. The poles included brave and powerful animals. Create your own totem pole.

Materials for each totem pole

- cardboard tube from wrapping paper, foil, paper towels, or plastic wrap
- colored paper
- scissors
- glue
- markers

Directions

1. Cut a piece of colored paper to cover the tube. Glue it in place.

2. Cut a strip for each animal and glue it around the tube. Each strip should be about two inches wide.

3. Think about the positive qualities certain animals represent, such as courage, strength, gentleness, or cleverness. Some possibilities include eagles, ravens, bears, foxes, and rabbits.

4. Use colored paper to add ears, wings, beaks, snouts, and teeth to the strips to form your chosen animals. To create wings, cover only the front of the tube with the strip. Fold the ends out on either side.

5. To add a snout or a beak, fold a strip of paper in half the long way. Cut it to a point for a beak or clip it to a more rounded shape for a snout. Fold down a tab on the flat end of the strip to glue it to the pole.

6. Draw additional details with the markers.

String Painting

Warm colors include red, yellow, and orange. Blue, green, and purple are cool colors. Experiment with the chillier hues in this wintry string abstract.

Materials

- white paper
- milk cartons or other wide-mouthed containers for the tempera
- blue tempera
- green tempera
- purple tempera
- three strips of cotton string, approximately 8″ long

Directions

1. Dip the string in blue paint.

2. Lay it in loops on the paper.

3. Experiment with pulling the string across the paper in different directions.

4. Let the blue paint dry.

5. Repeat with green.

6. Use the purple last.

7. Let some of the white paper show through.

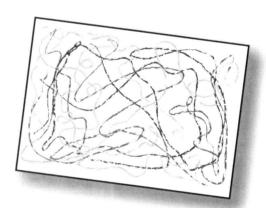

A Sphere of Circles

Flat circles turn three-dimensional in this festive project.

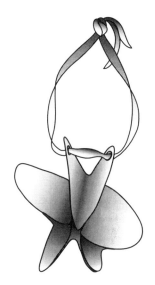

Materials

- round lid
- colored construction paper, white tagboard, or used greeting cards
- markers
- scissors
- glue
- hole punch
- narrow gift ribbon

Directions

1. Trace around the lid to draw six separate circles.

2. If you are using recycled greeting cards, cut out the circles. If you are using colored paper or white tagboard, decorate the circles with markers before you cut them out.

4. Fold each circle in half.

5. Glue half of the outside of first circle to half of the outside of the second circle. You will have a new circle with a fin sticking up in the middle.

6. Glue half of the outside of the third circle to half of the outside of the second circle.

7. Repeat until all six of the circles are used. Glue the sixth circle to the first one, then punch a hole through a "fin" on each side of the ball near the top.

8. Thread a piece of ribbon through the two holes and tie it to create a loop for hanging.

Gift Bags

The winter season is full of opportunities for giving, but these puzzling bags are good for any season.

Materials

- paper lunch sacks (preferably white)
- markers
- colored construction paper
- scissors
- glue

Directions

1. Cut a panel from one sheet of construction paper for the front of the sack. It should be the same width as the sack, but one or two inches shorter to allow the sack to fold at the top.

2. Draw question marks of all sizes on the panel. Make some large and some small, some fat and some thin.

3. Color some of the question marks with markers. Cut others out of foil wrapping paper or different colors of construction paper. Glue them down.

4. Glue the panel to the front of the sack.

5. Place your gift inside the sack, fold over the top and staple it shut.

Alternatives:

1. Create a design with the name of the gift's recipient.

2. Create a design based on the gift itself. The design should give clues but not reveal the contents.

Create a Robot

Wouldn't it be great to have a robot to help you clean your room before holiday guests arrive? This one won't really do any work, but he or she will be good for a laugh.

Materials for each robot:

- 2 wrapping paper tubes, narrow boxes, or straws for arms
- 2 narrow boxes or foam cups for legs
- medium-sized product box such as a cereal box
- smaller box for the head
- glue
- scissors
- tempera
- paintbrush
- buttons, paper cups, broken costume jewelry, parts of plastic water bottles, and other interesting junk for additional details

Directions

1. Glue the smaller box to the top of the larger one.

2. Attach the tube or box arms to your robot with paper fasteners, or simply glue them on.

3. Attach the narrow boxes or the foam cups to your robot for legs.

4. Glue the paper cups to your robot for ears, eyes, or other features.

5. Paint your robot, and add creative details.

Geometry Zoo

When the weather turns stormy, it's a chance to switch on your imagination and create new worlds indoors. Make a whole zoo of wonderful animals out of colored paper shapes.

Materials

- colored construction paper
- scissors
- glue
- white copy paper
- shape patterns from the next page
- markers

Directions

1. Look at pictures of real animals. Which parts of their bodies remind you of circles? Which parts remind you of rectangles? Which parts remind you of triangles?

2. Cut out the pattern for the body shape that fits your animal best. For example, a cow's body could be a rectangle. Add more shapes for the head, legs, nose, eyes, and ears.

3. Write a riddle to go with your picture. For example, "I am not a cow. I say 'bow wow.'"

Geometry Zoo Shapes

Half a Face

Drawing is a great way to spend a winter afternoon. Use magazine pictures to draw faces.

Materials

- magazines, newspapers, catalogs, junk mail
- glue
- scissors
- white copy paper or drawing paper

Directions

1. Find a full-page picture of a face

2. Cut it out.

3. Cut it in half so there is one eye, half a nose, half a mouth, and half a chin.

4. Give the other half of the magazine picture to a friend.

5. Glue your half-face to the white paper.

6. With a pencil, carefully copy the details of the picture in reverse. Recreate the whole face. Remember to include the shadows.

Extension: Have a member of your group pose for the class. Your model will face the chalkboard. Draw his or her back.

Red Spirals on Green

The colors of the holiday season are complementary. Red and green are on opposite sides of the color wheel. Put them together and watch them vibrate.

Materials

- one 8½" x 11" sheet each of red and green construction paper
- scissors
- glue
- spiral pattern from the next page

Directions

1. Use the pattern to cut a spiral out of the red paper.

2. Glue it down on the green paper.

3. Try to look at your design!

Variation: Paint a sheet of paper evenly with red tempera. Let it dry. With a brush, splatter dots of green tempera on top of the red surface.

Spiral Pattern

Silhouettes

Etienne de Silhouette was an official in the court of King Louis XV of France. He also liked to create the profile portraits that are named after him. Try drawing one of your own.

Materials

- white copy paper
- 4″ x 6″ sheet of black construction paper
- scissors
- glue
- pencil
- newsprint or other sketching paper

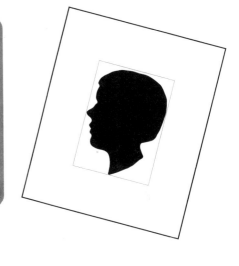

Directions

1. Choose a partner.

2. Lay the black construction paper down in the middle of the sketching paper. Trace around it to make a frame. Set the black paper aside.

3. Pose for your partner. Let your friend draw a side view of your head. The drawing should touch each side of the frame on the sketching paper. It should include your whole head, not just your face.

4. Switch places. This time you will draw, and your partner will pose. Don't worry about drawing eyes or ears. Just look at the outside shape.

5. Cut out the profile head.

6. Use it as a pattern to cut a profile head out of black paper.

7. Glue your silhouette down on the white paper.

Alternative: Aim a strong light at a piece of paper fastened to the wall. Have your partner sit so that his or her profile casts a distinct shadow on the paper. Trace around the shadow, and then use it as a pattern to create a silhouette.

Four-Pointed Stars

On long winter nights, the stars seem close enough to touch. Is it any wonder that people from all over the world use stars for decorations? Native American stars often had four points instead of five. Dark and light are called "values" in art. Create a three-dimensional effect by using a dark and a light color on this four-pointed star.

Materials

- star pattern from the next page
- crayons or colored markers
- pencils
- rulers

Directions

1. Using the ruler and a pencil, finish the pattern.

2. Color it with one dark and one light color. Examples are dark red and pink, dark blue and pale blue, dark brown and tan.

3. Alternate the colors.

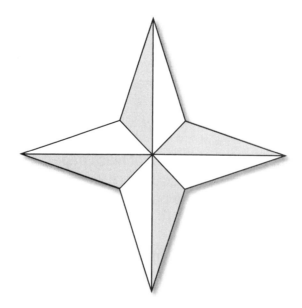

Four-Pointed Star Pattern

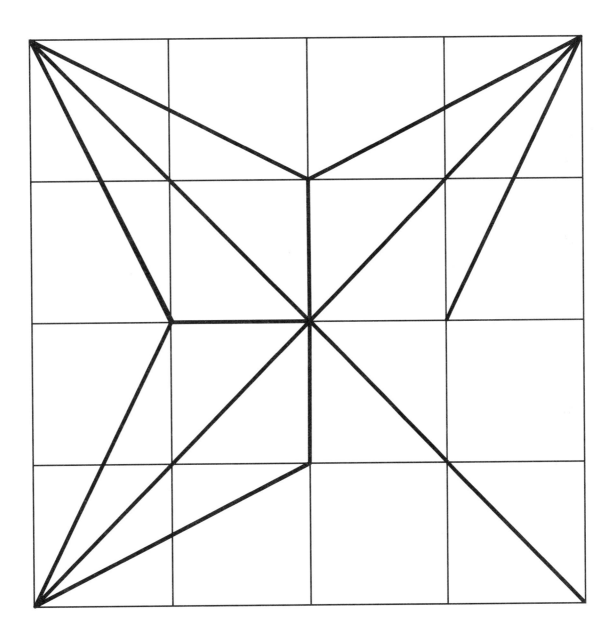

Make a Dreidel

Chanukah, or the Festival of Lights, is a Jewish holiday celebrated in late November or early December. It commemorates the rededication of the temple after the Jewish people defeated their Syrian oppressors more than 2,300 years ago. Chanukah lasts eight days because a small amount of oil burned for eight days instead of just one when the temple was rededicated. During Chanukah, children play with a special top called a *dreidel*. Make one of your own.

Materials

- Bristol board or light tagboard
- scissors
- pencil
- markers
- dreidel pattern from the next page

Directions

1. Cut out the pattern. The dashed lines indicate the tabs.

2. Trace it onto the piece of Bristol board or light tagboard and cut out the dreidel.

3. Draw one of these Hebrew letters on each side of the dreidel:

   gimel   hey   nun   shin

They stand for the words "a great miracle happened there."

4. Fold the dreidel, and apply glue to the tabs.

5. Push a sharpened pencil through the top. The tip will stick out of the dreidel's pointed end.

6. The eraser end of the pencil is the handle. Give your dreidel a spin.

Extension: Dreidels are used to play a game. Look up the rules online or in the library.

Dreidel Pattern

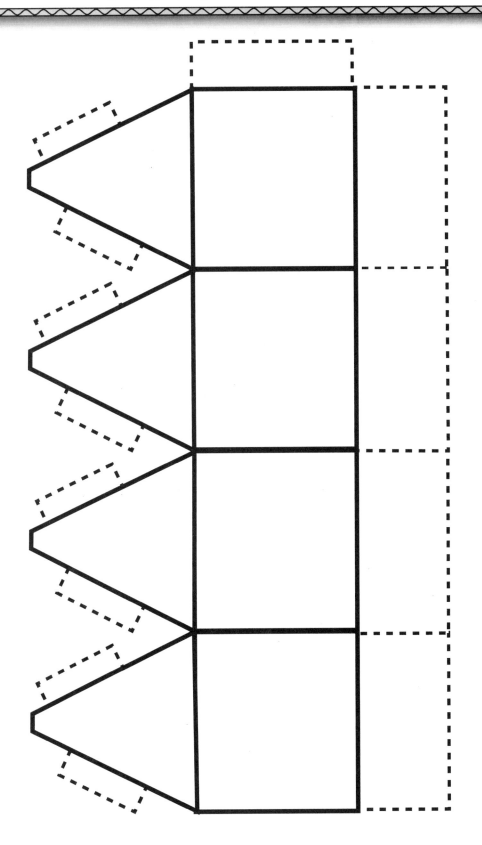

Rose Windows

Gothic cathedrals were made of stone. The ceilings were very high. Round windows set with stained glass brought light inside. Like the designs in a kaleidoscope, rose windows were symmetrical. Finish the rose window design, and then use four colors, plus black, to complete the symmetry.

Materials

- colored markers, black markers
- rose window pattern from the next page
- pencils
- black construction paper
- scissors
- glue
- colored tissue paper

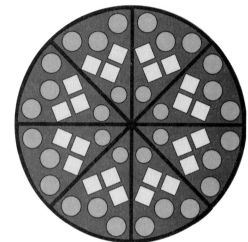

Directions

1. Using the rose window pattern on the next page, notice how the pattern of circles and diamonds in each pie-shaped section is repeated in the next pie-shaped section. Use the same pattern to complete the other six sections.

2. Color all of the small circles near the center of the "window" the same color. Create a pattern with the rest of the colors in the first section.

3. Repeat the same color pattern in the other seven sections.

4. Make the space around the colored circles and triangles black.

5. Tape your design to a window.

Alternative:

1. Select your own repeating shapes.

2. Cut the shapes out of a round piece of black construction paper.

3. Glue tissue paper behind the cutouts.

4. Tape your design to a window.

Rose Window Pattern

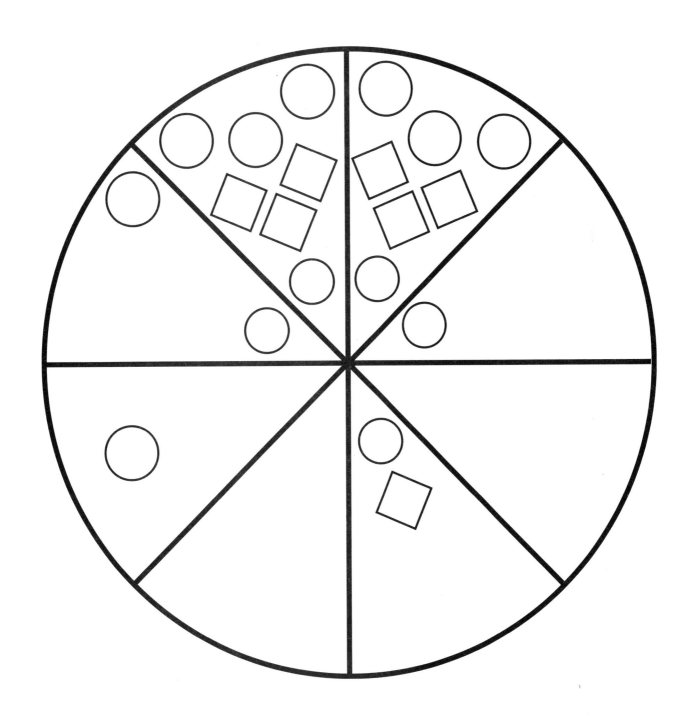

Block Print Greeting Cards

Print a special card for someone who lives far away. This winter tradition is a great way to keep in touch.

Materials for each card

- 5" x 7" flat section from a foam meat tray
- pencil
- scissors
- undiluted liquid tempera
- spoon
- 5" x 7" sheet of white paper for the print
- 8½" x 11" sheet of colored construction paper for the card
- flat tempera brush or a printer's brayer

Directions

1. Fold the colored paper in half, short end to short end, to make a card.

2. Draw designs or pictures on the smooth side of the foam. Press hard enough to leave indentations, but not hard enough to make holes.

4. Use the brush or brayer to spread paint evenly on the surface of the tray. The indented lines will stay white.

5. Lay the white paper on top of the block. Rub across the back of the paper with a spoon.

6. Peel the paper off of the block.

7. Let the paint dry.

8. Glue the finished print to the front of the card.

Draw   **Ink**   **Trim & Glue to Card**

70

Holiday Gift Wrap: Spatter Painting

There are many great ways to create designs on paper. This one, inspired by abstract expressionist Jackson Pollock, is fast and fun.

Materials

- giftwrap-sized sheet of paper (This can be bond craft paper from a large roll or tissue paper. You might want to experiment first with recycled paper such as newspaper or a brown paper grocery sack.)
- tempera
- newspaper or tarps to protect the workspace
- old oversized shirts to protect clothing
- toothbrush or other stiff brush for each color
- square of window screen wire for each color (Protect the edges with tape.)

Directions

1. Spread the paper out flat on the protected work surface.

2. Dip the toothbrush or other stiff brush into the paint.

3. Hold the screen over the paper.

4. Rub the brush across the screen to spatter the color onto the paper.

5. Repeat with another color.

Caution: Do not let the paint get too thick or your design will crack when you wrap the gift.

6. Allow the decorated paper to dry.

Stamp Keeper

Make a handy gift for an adult friend or relative. This little portfolio fits neatly into a glove compartment or briefcase to keep postage stamps handy.

Materials for each stamp keeper

- one sheet of white copy paper or other 8½″ x 11″ paper
- glue
- markers
- pictures of international postage stamps
- ruler
- pencil
- *optional:* clear, self-adhesive shelf paper

Directions

1. Turn the paper so the long edge faces you (landscape mode).

2. Measure and make a mark three inches from the bottom of the paper on the left and on the right. Draw a line between the marks.

3. Fold up a flap along the line.

4. Fold the paper in half to form a small portfolio with two pockets inside.

5. Measure and mark one inch from the left edge at both the top and bottom. Draw a line between the marks and fold in a flap. Glue it down. Repeat on the right side of the portfolio.

6. Decorate the outside of the stamp keeper with stamps you invent. Look at photos of real stamps for ideas. Stamps can have pictures of animals, flowers, places, and famous people. They include the name of the country and the amount of postage the stamp is worth. Your stamps can be realistic or totally imaginative. It's up to you.

7. (Optional) Cover the outside of your decorated stamp keeper with clear, self-adhesive shelf paper so it will last longer.

Alternative: Save canceled stamps from regular mail and collage them onto the cover and the inside pocket.

A Reminder Book

Create a reminder book as a gift for someone special.

Materials for one book

- Bristol board, cover, or other light cardstock $8\frac{1}{2}''$ x $5\frac{1}{2}''$
- Three $8\frac{1}{2}''$ x $5\frac{1}{2}''$ sheets of copy paper
- stapler
- markers
- scratch paper
- pencil
- *optional:* clear, self-adhesive shelf paper

Directions

1. Using the scratch paper, plan a design using the elements of a clock face: the numerals 1–12, a minute hand, an hour hand, and the outside circle shape.

2. Fold the Bristol board in half to form the booklet cover. Draw your design on the front. Cover with self-adhesive shelf paper if desired.

3. Fold the pages in half.

4. Staple the book together. Use two or three staples on the fold.

Holiday Tetrahedrons

Make one (or a dozen) of these geometric decorations.

Materials

- index, cover, or cardstock
- markers
- scissors
- thin ribbon for hanging
- tetrahedron pattern from the next page
- glue
- *optional:* glitter glue

Directions

1. Cut out the pattern.

2. Trace the pattern onto cardstock.

3. Use a ruler to draw the fold lines.

4. Decorate the blank space inside each triangle.

5. Cut out the tetrahedron.

6. Fold inward on the fold lines.

7. Spread glue evenly onto the flaps.

8. Glue the tetrahedron together.

Tetrahedron Pattern

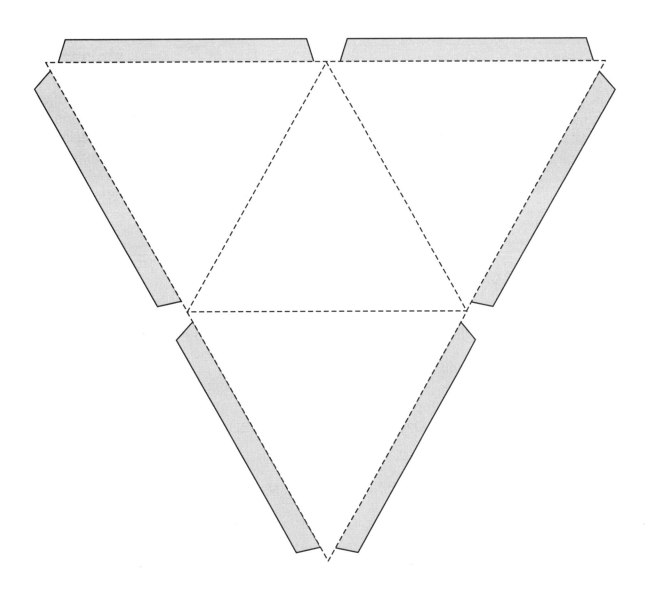

Op Art Paper Weaving in Red and Green

This wild and wavy project is sure to leave you blinking.

Materials

- one 9″ x 12″ sheet each of red and green construction paper
- scissors
- glue
- ruler
- pencil

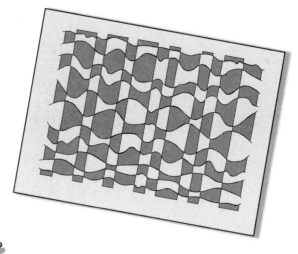

Directions

1. Draw a line one inch from each edge of the red construction paper.

2. Fold the red paper in half, short edge to short edge.

3. Draw wavy lines from the top line to the fold. Draw enough lines to go all the way across the paper. (Similar to Rainy Day Placemats on page 12, but with wavy rather than straight cuts.)

4. Cut the green paper into straight $\frac{1}{2}″$ and 1″ strips. Make some of the strips wide and some of them narrow.

5. Weave each straight green strip over and under alternate wavy cuts in the red paper. If one row starts "over," start the next one "under." The narrow and wide strips will create different effects.

6. Glue the ends in place so the weaving does not come apart.

Extension: Create more complicated designs by grouping very narrow strips and wider strips. The wavy cuts may also be planned more carefully for special effects.

Snip Out Some Flakes!

Fill your bulletin board, cover your windows, or hang these lacy beauties from your ceiling for a papery winter wonderland.

Materials for each snowflake

- white copy paper
- scissors
- protractor or protractor pattern on the next page
- *optional:* snowflake patterns on the next page
- ruler

Directions

1. With the paper in portrait orientation, flat on the desk, lift the lower right corner. Bring the entire short edge of the paper over to meet the long edge and fold along the resulting angle. You will have a triangle with a rectangular flap at the top. Cut off the flap.

2. Use a ruler to find the center of the diagonal fold at the base of the triangle.

3. Cut out the protractor. Place it on the fold with the center dot on the center mark.

4. Mark 60° and 120° on the copy paper.

5. Draw a line from the center point on the fold to the 60° mark. Repeat with the 120° mark.

6. Fold inward along each line. One flap will overlap the other.

7. Cut out small chunks from each fold. Cutting off the point will create a hole in the middle. The more small chunks you cut off, the lacier your snowflake will be. Use the snowflake patterns on the next page if you wish.

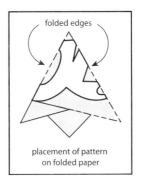

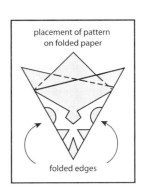

8. Unfold and enjoy!

Protractor and Snowflake Patterns

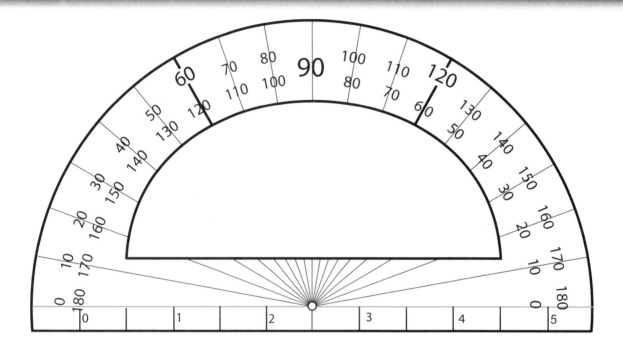

Trace patterns onto folded paper; place gray lines along folded edges; cut along dotted lines.

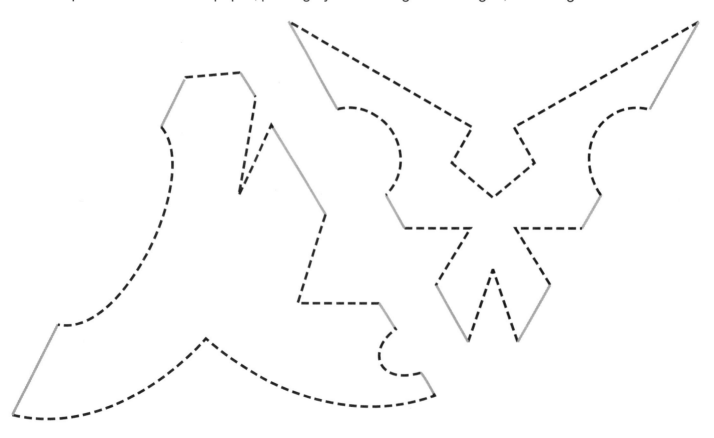

Wreath Double Reversals

Use these vibrant complementary colors to create a symmetrical wreath design.

Materials

- one sheet 9" x 12" red paper
- one sheet 9" x 6" green paper
- scissors
- glue
- pencil

Directions

1. Draw half of a wreath on the green paper. It should fill most of the paper without touching any edge except the right side. Imagine that the right edge of the paper is a fold.

2. Cut out the half of a wreath. It should be shaped like half of a doughnut with uneven edges to suggest evergreen boughs.

3. Save all of the pieces.

4. Lay the green paper that was around the wreath on the left side of the red paper. Match the straight edges.

5. Lay the cut-out wreath half opposite the hole, creating a wreath shape that is half red and half green.

6. Lay the green center section from the middle of the wreath back on the left side of the picture, opposite the cutout of the center section, completing the wreath.

7. Cut a bow shape out of the green wreath half. Reverse the green bow piece onto the red half of the wreath.

8. Glue all of the pieces in place.

Apples and Oranges: Crayon Etching

Holiday tables are bright with seasonal fruits. Crayon etching makes this still life glow.

Materials for one crayon etching

- newspapers or a tarp to protect the table
- heavy paper, cardstock, or cereal box cardboard
- crayons   • paper clip
- black watercolor marker
- pencil   • ruler

Directions

1. Draw several large apples and oranges.

2. Trace over the pencil lines with black marker.

3. Color in the apples and oranges with crayons. Color the background also. Press hard to lay down bright, rich wax color.

4. Color over the entire picture with black crayon.

5. Use the ruler and the straightened paper clip to scratch straight parallel lines all the way across the black crayon surface revealing the picture underneath. The lines may be vertical, horizontal, or diagonal, but they should be straight and should continue all the way across the page.

Extension: Reveal more of the picture by using hatching. Scratch vertical lines all the way across the picture, then repeat with horizontal and diagonal lines. Hatching is also used to create darks in pencil drawings and in ink drawings.

A

B

Ring in the New Year!

The artist M.C. Escher created fascinating interlocking drawings. When you look at his paintings, it is hard to tell where one bird or fish ends and the next one begins. This kind of design is called a "tessellation." Create a tessellation with a holiday theme.

Materials

- bell pattern from the next page
- pencil
- markers: black, yellow, and orange
- scissors
- copies of the reproducible worksheet from the next page

Directions

1. Cut out the bell pattern.

2. A partial row of bells on the worksheet has been completed. Notice how they interlock. One bell is right-side-up, and the other is upside-down.

3. Use the pattern to draw the missing bells on the worksheet.

4. Color the design so that no two adjacent bells are yellow.

5. Trace over the lines with black marker.

Ring in the New Year Patterns

Reproducible Bell Pattern

Worksheet

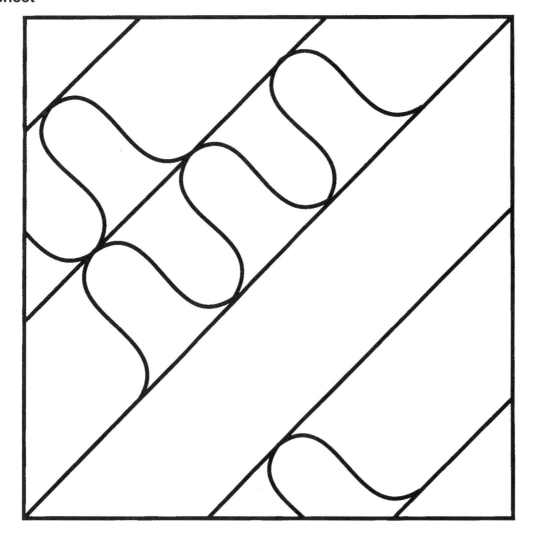

Painted Clay Animals

Create miniature animals with salt and flour clay, and then paint them with tempera hues inspired by a Mexican fiesta.

Materials

- table salt
- flour
- water
- container to use to mix the clay
- tempera or student acrylic
- *optional:* pictures of traditional Mexican designs

Directions

1. Mix one part salt with one part flour. Add water a little at a time to form moldable clay. If the mixture is too sticky, sprinkle in flour.

2. Form the clay into an animal shape.

3. Let it dry completely. Larger animals will take longer to dry than small animals.

4. Paint the animal a bright color. Add designs such as hearts, stars, or geometric patterns with a small brush, if desired. Use colors and designs inspired by a Mexican fiesta.

Extension: Create a decorative animal piñata out of a grocery sack. Glue fringed strips of crepe paper or tissue paper around all four sides of the sack. Glue the first strip around the bottom. Glue the next strip just above and overlapping it. Repeat to cover the sack. Add eyes, a nose, and a mouth or a beak with colored paper. Visit the library or Internet to see pictures of authentic piñatas.

Matisse's Birthday: Colored Paper Cutouts

The painter Henri Matisse, born on December 31, 1869, was a master of color and design. In addition to drawings, prints, and oil paintings on canvas, he created bright abstracts with cut paper. Make your own cut-paper masterpieces.

Materials

- colored construction paper sheets, cut in half to $4\frac{1}{2}''$ x $5\frac{1}{2}''$
- heavy drawing paper
- scissors
- glue
- *optional:* reproductions of paper cutouts by Henri Matisse

Directions

1. Choose three different colors. One should be much darker or lighter that the other two. For example, pink, pale yellow, and dark purple. The darker or lighter color is for contrast.

2. Cut abstract shapes out of the paper. Cut shapes with no angles and no straight edges.

3. Arrange the shapes on the drawing paper.

4. Glue them in place.

Extension: Use hand-decorated papers created by spatter painting, wet-on-wet painting, block printing, fingerpaint monoprints, or string printing. You may also wish to include shapes cut from recycled gift wrap, newspaper want ads, grocery bags, tissue paper, or colored paper. Matisse used white paper that had been painted on one side by an assistant.

Envelope Calendar

Hang this special calendar on a nail. It will keep tickets and other small items handy all year. It's also a great way to use recycled mailing envelopes.

Materials for each calendar

- mailing envelope (9″ x 12″ or larger)
- sheet of colored construction paper to fit the envelope
- twelve-month calendar created on the computer and printed half the size of the construction paper; staple pages together along top edge
- gummed or self-adhesive reinforcement
- half a sheet of white copy paper
- glue
- markers

Directions

1. Glue the construction paper to the front of the envelope. (This will cover the address if the envelope is recycled.)

2. Glue the calendar on the lower half of the construction paper.

3. Use a ruler to divide the plain white paper into four sections. Draw pictures to represent the four seasons.

4. Glue the picture page to the construction paper above the calendar.

5. Punch a hole in the envelope flap if there is none.

6. Add a gummed or self-adhesive reinforcement.

7. Hang the calendar where you can check it daily.

Kwanzaa Accordion Book

Books are given as gifts during Kwanzaa, a seven-day celebration of African tradition and culture that begins on December 26. Make a book of your own to recognize the seven principles of Kwanzaa: Unity, Self-Determination, Collective Work and Responsibility, Cooperative Economics, Purpose, Creativity, and Faith.

Materials for each book

- one sheet of copy paper or index stock
- 3" x 5" construction paper in red or green
- pencil and pen
- thin ribbon in red, green, or black
- glue
- black marker
- ruler

Directions

1. Measure off one-inch intervals on each short side of the copy paper, and then draw lines one inch apart across the page. These will serve as guidelines for the printed words.

2. Fold the paper in half the long way, creating a double strip.

3. Bring the short sides of the strip together to fold it in half.

4. Fold each short side to meet the center fold, creating an accordion or fan book with four pages on each side. The first section, with folds on the top and the left side, is the cover.

5. Glue the construction paper to the cover.

6. Neatly print "Kwanzaa" on the cover, and print a principle on each page.

7. Tie a ribbon around the finished book. Black, red, and green are the colors of Kwanzaa.

a.

b.
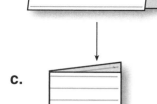

c.
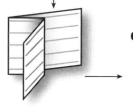

d.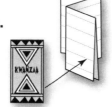

e.

f.

g.

Presidents' Day: Lincoln in Scale

Artists have used scaling to enlarge sketches since the days of the old masters. Use this classic method to draw a larger version of the Lincoln portrait at the bottom of the page.

Materials

- paper
- ruler
- pencil
- eraser
- drawing of Lincoln on a 2″ by 2″ grid with lines every $\frac{1}{2}$ inch

Directions

1. Draw a 4″ x 4″ square on your paper

2. Mark off every inch on both sides.

3. Use a ruler to connect each set of marks.

4. Copy the details of each section of the small drawing into the matching section of the larger drawing.

Extension: Enlarge the picture to fit a 16″ x 16″ grid. Draw grids on photocopies of other presidential portraits and enlarge them for the bulletin board. The Internet has many historic public domain drawings.

A Mystery Drawing

How well can you copy the drawing on the next page?

Materials

- paper
- copy of the mystery drawing for each student or a transparency made from the mystery drawing, projected. The copies should be on the table when the students come in so the true subject is not obvious.
- pencils
- erasers

Directions

1. Carefully copy each detail.

2. Turn the drawing 90° counterclockwise to discover the drawing's mystery subject.

A Mystery Drawing Pattern

Copy This Drawing

Be an Inventor

Thomas Alva Edison was born on February 11, 1847. His inventions, which include the electric light, have changed the world. In his honor, February 11 has been declared National Inventors' Day. Exercise your creativity. Just for today, be an inventor.

Materials

- recycled items such as product boxes, tubes, foil, wire, bottle tops, bottoms from plastic water or soda bottles, and scraps of fabric
- inexpensive disposable items such as yarn, crepe paper, paper plates, paper cups, flexible drinking straws, plastic forks, spoons, and knives
- chenille stems, wire coat hangers, large paper clips
- paper punch, glue, tape, staples, and stapler
- colored construction paper
- markers
- magazines, catalogs, and junk mail for collage
- tempera, white indoor latex paint, or gesso

Directions

1. Pick one item to be the basis of the invention. It could be a box or a pair of paper plates glued together. It could be a coat hanger bent into an unusual shape.

2. Paint this item with tempera, white indoor latex paint, or gesso to cover any product information. (You may choose to cover it with a collaged design, aluminum foil, or construction paper instead of paint.)

3. Glue other items onto your prepared shape. For example, you might add bottle tops as knobs. You might draw instrument dials with markers. You might add water bottle bottoms to the sides for observation windows.

Extension: Give your invention a name. Look up a real patent application online. Write a patent application for your invention.

Alternatives: Draw or paint a picture of your invention instead of creating a three-dimensional model, or draw a picture of a commonly used invention such as a safety pin, a paper clip, or a button.

Stained Glass Butterflies

These beautiful butterflies will brighten your windows or walls.

Materials for each butterfly

- two 9" x 12" sheets of black construction paper
- colored tissue paper
- scissors
- glue
- butterfly pattern from the next page

Directions

1. Cut out the butterfly pattern.

2. Fold the construction paper in half, matching the short edges.

3. Place the "body" edge of the pattern on the fold.

4. Trace around the pattern and cut out two copies of the black butterfly framework.

5. Glue colored tissue behind each opening in the wings on one of the copies.

6. Glue the other black butterfly outline piece on the back, covering the edges of the tissue.

Extensions:

1. Find pictures of real butterflies online or in the library. Create your own design based on the pattern of an actual butterfly wing.

2. Make your butterfly very small. Glue a magnet on the body. Use it to hold notes on the refrigerator door.

Butterfly Pattern

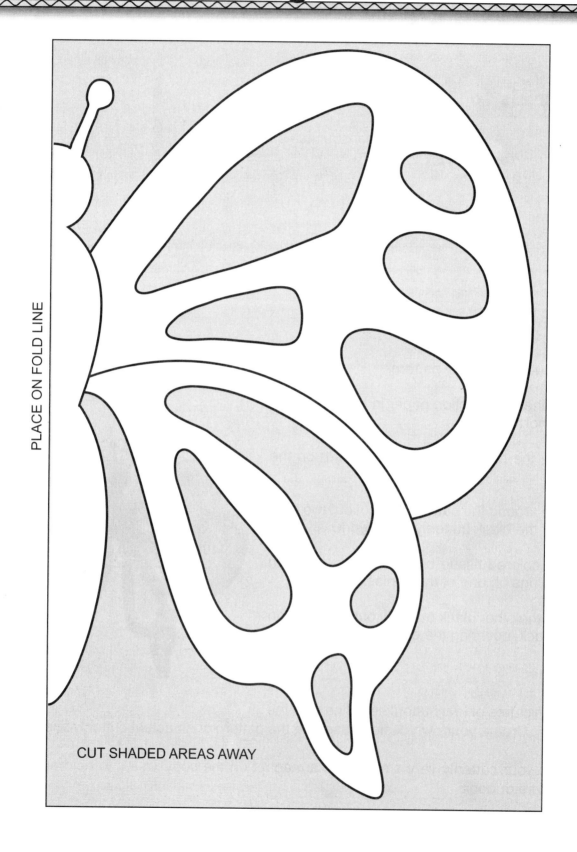

PLACE ON FOLD LINE

CUT SHADED AREAS AWAY

Chinese New Year: Invent a Dragon

Asian dragons are not evil. As symbols of good fortune, they are included in many New Year's celebrations. Invent a lucky dragon of your own.

Materials for a dragon scroll

- copy paper, legal size
- two dowels, cardboard strips, or cardboard tubes (Each one should be the width of the paper plus 2 inches.)
- pencil
- colored pencils or markers
- glue
- red ribbon, string, or yarn for hanging
- *optional:* colored bond, foil paper, or wrapping paper with an Asian graphic, one inch larger than the copy paper on all sides

Directions

1. Study pictures of Asian dragons.

2. Turn the paper so it is in portrait mode. In pencil, draw your own dragon on the copy paper. Let your dragon fill the page with its head near the bottom and its tail near the top. Leave about an inch at the top and bottom free.

3. Color your dragon with colored pencils or markers.

4. Turn the drawing over so the blank side is up. Center the dowel over the page about one inch down from the top edge.

5. Fold the top edge over the dowel and glue in place.

6. Repeat at the bottom edge with the other dowel.

7. *Optional:* Glue the legal bond to a slightly larger sheet of colored bond, foil paper, or wrapping paper with an Asian motif before attaching the dowels.

8. Tie the ribbon or yarn to both ends of the top dowel for hanging.

9. To store, roll from both ends to create a scroll.

Alternate: Create a dragon from half an egg carton. Use each egg cup as a section of the dragon's body. Cut the tail, legs, ears, and horns from cereal box cardboard and glue them on. Paint your dragon with tempera or acrylic.

Chinese Lanterns—Paper Cutting

Create festive paper lanterns for a Chinese New Year celebration.

Materials

- red construction paper or index-weight paper
- scissors
- glue, cellophane tape, or staples
- ruler
- pencil
- string or red gift ribbon for hanging
- string
- paper clips

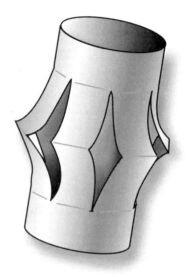

Directions

1. Measure off and draw border lines 1–2 inches from each edge of the red paper.

2. With the paper in landscape orientation, start to measure at the one-inch line, and mark off every two inches across the top. Repeat across the bottom. Using a ruler, draw lines between the dots.

3. Fold the paper in half, matching the long edges.

4. Cut along each line, starting at the fold and ending at the border line.

5. Unfold.

6. Glue the short sides together to form a lantern shape. The fold should bend outward.

7. Hold the cylinder together with paper clips until the glue dries.

8. Push down on the top of the cylinder to open out the cuts and create a lantern shape.

9. Punch holes and attach string or red gift ribbon at the top for hanging.

Note: These paper "lanterns" are for decoration only. Do not use them with candles, light bulbs, or any other heat source.

Playing Card Banner (King or Queen of Hearts)

For Valentine's Day, make yourself into the King or Queen of Hearts.

Materials for each banner

- playing card or a picture of the king or queen of hearts
- one sheet of $8\frac{1}{2}$" x 11" drawing paper
- pencil
- markers
- 24" piece of red yarn

Directions

1. In portrait orientation, center the top of the drawing paper on the piece of red yarn.

2. Fold $\frac{1}{2}$" of paper over the yarn and glue it in place. Yarn will stick out on either side, so the completed banners can be tied together.

3. Copy the king or queen of hearts or another favorite playing card character. Notice that you have to copy the figure twice. Also notice how the two figures on the card join in the middle.

4. As you draw, change the clothes and symbols on the card to match your own interests. Leave both faces blank.

5. Use the mirror to draw your own face in the blanks.

6. If you do not have a mirror, copy a photograph of your face.

7. Tie the banners together and display them around the room.

Extension:
1. On two large sheets of tagboard or recycled cardboard, draw clothes based on the outfit worn by the king or queen of hearts. Add color using markers or cut paper. Punch holes in the top of each piece of cardboard. Loop string through the holes and tie to create a "sandwich-board" costume.

2. Write a short play about playing cards that talk. Use the costumes to act it out. Read "Alice in Wonderland" for ideas.

Mom's Valentine's Day Card

This traditional favorite is sure to find a place on Mom's dresser.

Materials

- small paper doily or delicate snowflake design (See "Snip Out Some Flakes!" on page 78.)
- two sheets of red construction paper
- magazines, catalogs, and junk mail items that include flower pictures
- thin red ribbon tied in miniature bows
- white paper
- black marker

Directions

1. Fold the red paper in half to form the card.

2. Glue the doily to the front of the card. (The fold of the card will be on the left side.)

3. Cut a heart out of the other sheet of red paper. It should be smaller than the doily.

4. Glue it in the center of the doily.

5. Cut a smaller white heart. Glue it in the center of the red heart.

6. Cut a small picture of a flower from a catalog or magazine and glue it in the middle of the white heart.

7. Glue the miniature bow under the flower.

8. Use the black marker to write a message inside, or write a message on a 4″ x 5″ sheet of white paper and glue it inside.

Mondrian's Birthday

The Dutch painter Piet Mondrian was born on March 7, 1872. He was part of a group of artists who wanted to create an artistic language everyone could understand. They used only the primary colors of red, yellow, and blue, plus black and white. They assembled their compositions with straight lines, squares, and rectangles. Create a painting in the style of Mondrian.

Materials

- paper for tempera painting (white, if possible)
- red, yellow, blue, black, and white tempera
- tempera brushes
- ruler
- pencil
- *optional:* reproductions of Mondrian paintings

Directions

1. Draw one large rectangle or square on the left side of the paper, and then draw one medium and several small squares or rectangles on the right side.

2. Paint each of the rectangles or squares with a primary color. Let them dry.

3. Outline each square or rectangle with black paint. Let the black paint dry.

4. If you did not use white paper, fill in the remaining surface with white paint.

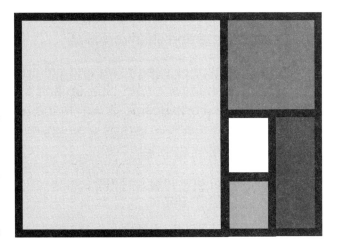

Shamrock Repetitive Design

Repeated designs are everywhere. Look for them on walls, floors, and fabrics. Create a repeated design with an Irish attitude in honor of St. Patrick's Day.

Materials

- shamrock pattern
- pale and dark green sheets of construction paper
- white drawing paper or copy paper
- pencils
- scissors
- glue

Directions

1. Cut out the shamrock pattern.

2. Trace around it 16 times on dark green paper.

3. Cut out the green shamrocks.

4. Arrange them in even rows and columns. Turn one shamrock right-side-up and then turn the next one upside-down. In the next row, if the one above is right-side-up, make the one below upside-down.

5. Glue the alternating shamrocks down on the light green paper.

Extension: Cut half of the shamrocks out of light green paper. Glue them to white or yellow paper instead of green. Create a more complex pattern using the two colors, as well as reversals.

Shamrock Pattern:

Homage to Josef Albers

Printmaker and designer Josef Albers, who was born March 19, 1888, created a series of famous lithographs called "Homage to the Square." In this series, he explored the interrelationships between shape and color. Celebrate his spring birthday by mixing up some tints and creating your own homage to the square.

Materials for each square

- tempera, one primary color
- tempera, white
- painting paper
- paintbrush
- ruler
- pencil
- foam meat tray or the lid of a foam egg carton (for mixing)
- *optional:* reproductions of "Homage to the Square"

Directions

1. Measure, and then draw a large square on the paper.

2. Draw another square inside the first one.

3. Draw two more squares, each one inside the last.

4. Paint the innermost square with a pure color such as red.

5. In the mixing tray, mix some of the pure color with white. Paint the space between the third and fourth squares with the mixture.

6. Add more white. Paint the space between the second and third squares with the mixture.

7. Add more white. Paint the space between the first and second squares with the mixture. Take your time painting. Practice controlling your brush.

Extension: Paint another square using the same colors, but reversing the order. Paint the center white, then add more red with each square, moving outward. Notice which part of each square seems to come forward and which part seems to go back.

Laughing Guy Tessellation

Does April Fool's Day make you laugh? Complete and color this laughing guy tessellation.

Materials

- laughing guy pattern from the next page
- tessellation worksheet on the next page
- pencil
- markers

Directions

1. Use the pattern to draw the rest of the design on the page. You will need to turn the pattern over every other time.

2. Use markers to make every other "laughing guy" a different color. Use two or four colors. Repeat the color pattern.

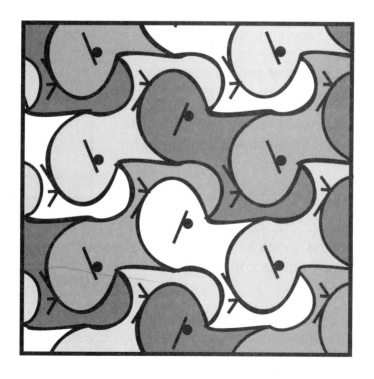

Laughing Guy Pattern and Worksheet

Pattern

Worksheet

Design a Clown Face

Every day is April Fool's Day for a clown. The makeup and clothes are funny because they exaggerate normal features and apparel. Practice exaggeration by designing makeup for a clown face.

Materials for each clown face

- paper
- crayons
- pencil
- eraser
- *optional:* pictures of clowns

Directions

1. Draw a large oval. Add eyes, eyebrows, a nose, a mouth, and ears to make a face.

2. Exaggerate each feature by adding one or more shapes around it in pencil. For example, an eye could have a large oval around it and a diamond inside the oval.

3. Add silly hair and a hat. The hat could be very large, very small, or it could have goofy details such as feathers, flowers, or fruit. The hair could be very curly, in braids, or it could stick out in all directions.

4. Draw a silly collar and add a scarf or tie.

5. Color your clown face. Use bright colors. Leave some parts of the face white.

Extension: Make a paper plate mask or a paper bag puppet using the clown picture as a pattern.

Earth Day: Draw a Habitat

The place where an animal lives is its habitat. A habitat has everything an animal needs to survive. For example, a shark's habitat is the ocean. Draw a real or imaginary animal and its habitat.

Materials

- drawing paper
- markers, crayons, colored pencils, watercolor or tempera paints
- pencil
- encyclopedias, library books, or the Internet

Directions

1. Choose an animal.

2. Find out about its needs, if you do not already know. Get ideas for what to include in your picture by consulting references. Even if your beast is imaginary, photographs of real places can give you ideas.

3. Draw your animal. Be sure to include its food and shelter in the picture. Add color with crayons, colored pencils, markers, and watercolor or tempera.

Optional: Study the award-winning picture book *Ashanti to Zulu: African Traditions* by Margaret W. Musgrove. Notice how the food, shelter, and general environment of each group of people is shown. This book is a great example of the kind of research many illustrators do.

Create a Planet

Of all the planets in our solar system, only Earth seems to be inhabited, but there are millions of other solar systems in the universe. Create your own inhabited planet.

Materials

- paper
- pencil
- crayons
- pictures of planets and "aliens"

Directions

1. Draw an "alien."

2. Draw his friends, his pets, his house, his transporter, and anything else in his environment.

3. Draw several moons in the sky.

Extension:

1. Write a story about your alien. Give him a name and a problem to solve. Name the planet and tell more about it. How long is each day? How does this affect the way your character lives? Are there seasons? How long do they last? How do your aliens learn?

2. You may wish to turn your story into an illustrated book. Use the stapled booklet style, the accordion book style, or look up hand bookbinding online or in the library.

Spring Flowers: Tissue Paper Collage

Bring spring indoors! Hang this flowery masterpiece in a dark corner.

Materials for one tissue collage

- white drawing paper or index-weight paper
- colored tissue in pastel colors plus purple, red, orange, and green
- scissors
- diluted white glue, starch, or clear acrylic medium
- tempera brush
- black marker

Directions

1. Cut flower shapes out of tissue.

2. Arrange the flower cutouts on the drawing paper.

3. Attach each cutout to the drawing paper by painting over it with starch, diluted glue, or acrylic medium. Place another cutout so that part of it overlaps one that has already been attached. Paint over it. Notice how the shapes show through and the colors blend. Use these effects to create your flower design.

Optional: Allow the collage to dry completely. With the marker, trace around the edges of shapes created by overlapping flowers.

Peach Blossoms: String and Sponge Print

Capture the beauty of an orchard in spring with this easy project. Use the completed picture to illustrate an original haiku.

Materials for each picture

- string
- household sponges cut into squares
- tempera in black or dark brown, white, and red
- meat tray or a foam egg carton lid for mixing paint
- paper for painting

Directions

1. Pour a small puddle of black or brown paint into the mixing tray.

2. Dip the string into the paint, and then pull it down and slightly to the right on the paper to create a branch.

3. Let it dry.

4. Pour a puddle of red and a puddle of white paint into the mixing tray.

5. Dip one edge of the sponge into white and the other edge into red. It's okay if they mix in the middle.

6. Use the end of the sponge to print four or five "petals" for each blossom. The flowers do not have to touch the branch. Some of them may overlap it.

7. When your peach blossom painting is finished, write a haiku to go along with it.

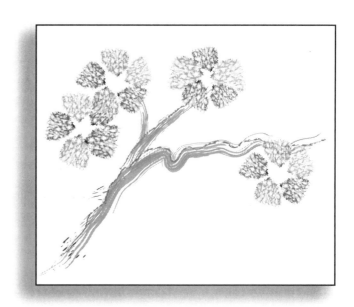

House of Clouds

Make a mysterious house of clouds. No matter which way you turn it, the roof points up.

Materials

- blue paper (*optional:* blue copy paper)
- sponges cut into small squares for printing
- white tempera
- pentagonal prism pattern from the next page
- ruler
- glue

Directions

1. Cut out the pattern.

2. Trace the pattern onto the blue paper or skip steps one through three and duplicate the page on blue copy paper.

3. Use the ruler to draw the fold lines on the blue paper.

4. Use the sponge and tempera to print clouds on the blue paper. Let the paint dry completely.

5. Cut out the blue pentagonal prism.

6. Spread glue on the tabs.

7. Fold inward along each fold line.

8. Glue the pentagonal prism together.

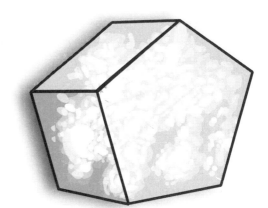

Optional: Poke two holes at the top and thread string or thin ribbon through them for hanging.

Extension: Enlarge the pattern on a photocopier or use the scaling technique. (See "Lincoln in Scale" on page 87.)

Pentagonal Prism Pattern

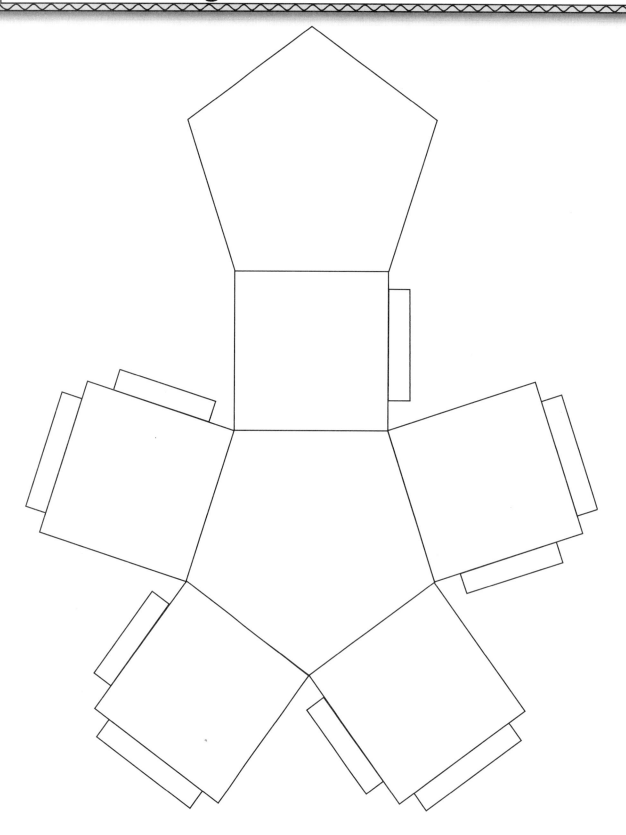

A Floral Watercolor

Use wet-on-wet watercolor to create a springtime classic. For best results, apply the lightest colors first.

Materials for each painting

- white paper for painting
- watercolors
- fine-line black markers or black pens
- water container
- watercolor brush

Optional: Set up a vase of backyard flowers or realistic artificial flowers in the center of a group of tables so that all students have a good view. For a large group, set up several vases.

Directions

1. Moisten the paint in each watercolor pan with a few drops of water.

2. Paint the front of the paper with clean water.

3. Touch the tip of the brush first to the yellow paint, then to two or three spots on the wet paper. The spot will bloom out in all directions.

4. Rinse the brush. Touch it to the orange paint, then to three other spots on the wet paper.

5. Repeat with the red paint. Work quickly.

6. Let the paint dry.

7. With the fine-line markers, draw the petals and other details. If not using a still-life set-up, check the library, garden catalogs, or the Internet for flower pictures.

Alternate: Cut the petals and the flower centers out of construction paper. Glue them to a sheet of green or blue paper. Make some of the flowers large and some of them small. Fill the page. Look at floral textile prints, wrapping paper, or wallpaper for ideas.

Surreal Pictures

Sigmund Freud, the father of psychoanalysis, was born May 6, 1856. His work influenced a group of artists and writers called "surrealists." They painted ideas and images that existed only in the human mind. Change ordinary magazine pictures into original works of surrealist art.

Materials

- magazines
- catalogs or junk mail
- scissors
- liquid glue or gluesticks
- drawing paper

Directions

1. Choose a backdrop from a magazine. The scene you select could be inside a room or outdoors. You may combine two or more pictures to create a weird setting for your picture.

2. Choose people or animals from different pictures. Cut them out. Combine parts from the pictures to create dream-like beings. They may have extra arms, eyes, or legs.

3. Add accessories such as umbrellas, scuba gear, or hats.

4. When you have finished arranging the picture, glue it down neatly, one piece at a time, starting with the backdrop.

Extension: Surrealists also used "automatic writing" to come up with new ideas. Look at your picture. Write the first word that comes into your mind, and then write a word that that word reminds you of. Keep writing as long as you can. Don't try to make this writing make sense. When you finish, put the paper away. After a week, take it out and read it. Write a poem or create a picture based on one phrase from the exercise. Throw the "automatic writing" paper away.

Exquisite Corpse

Some surrealists liked to play art games. One of their favorites was called "Exquisite Corpse." Have fun creating a unique work of art by committee.

Materials for each "Exquisite Corpse" drawing

- drawing paper or copy paper
- markers, crayons, or pencils
- group of four artists

Directions

1. Each member of the group should fan-fold a piece of paper into four sections.

2. On the front section, draw the head of a real or imaginary animal. Draw the neck so it runs over the fold on the right.

3. Continue a little bit of the neck on the next "page" so it will be easy to tell where to attach the body.

4. Fold the section back so only the second section is visible. Then pass it on to the next person.

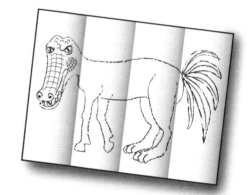

5. On the second section of the paper, starting with the neck, draw the front part of an animal's body, including the front legs and wings, if any.

6. Fold the section back and pass the paper to the next person. Draw the rear part of the body and hind legs on the third section of the paper.

7. Fold the section back, pass it on, and draw the tail on the fourth section of the paper.

8. Pass the paper one more time. Open the "Exquisite Corpse" drawings one at a time and share them with the group.

Note: Laughter is an important part of the game.

Black on White

The American abstract-Impressionist painter Franz Kline was born on May 23. He is famous for bold strokes of black paint on white canvases. Experience the exhilaration of bold brushwork with this quick painting.

Materials for each "black-on-white" painting

- large sheet of white paper
- wide, flat paintbrush
- black tempera in a wide-mouthed container, such as a milk carton
- reproductions of Franz Kline paintings and/or Zen ink paintings

Directions

1. Study the reproductions. Notice the energy in each stroke of black paint.

2. Dip the brush into the paint.

3. Make one bold stroke across the paper. Use your whole arm. Enjoy feeling "right" the first time.

4. Make two more strokes, and then put the painting aside to dry.

Make Tracks: Single Point Perspective

On May 10, 1869, the transcontinental railroad was finished. Tracks crossed the plains and mountains of the United States, and travel became easier for everyone. Practice single point perspective by drawing railroad tracks.

Note: If necessary, practice drawing parallel horizontal and parallel vertical lines before attempting this drawing.

Materials for each drawing

- copy paper
- ruler
- pencil

Directions

1. With the paper in "portrait" orientation, measure off and draw a horizontal line about one third down from the top of the paper.

2. Put a dot approximately in the center of that line.

3. Use the ruler to draw lines from each corner to that dot.

4. Use the ruler to draw horizontal lines between the lower diagonals. These will be the railroad ties. They should get closer together as they get closer to the dot and farther apart as they approach the bottom of the paper.

5. The top diagonal on the right is a telephone or telegraph line. Use the ruler to draw the poles. They must stay parallel to the side of the paper. Like the ties, the poles get closer together as they approach the dot and farther apart as they approach the side of the paper.

6. Add crosspieces to the telephone poles. Place the crosspiece where the wire crosses the pole. Each crosspiece must be parallel with the top and bottom edge of the paper.

7. Add hills to the distance and a road to the left side of the tracks. **Hint:** The two sides of the road also come together at the dot.

Japanese Windsocks

Hang these colorful windsocks on a porch to catch the spring breeze. They look best in a group, with some hanging high and others hanging low.

Materials

- colored paper in light or pastel colors
- crepe paper streamers or tissue paper cut into narrow strips
- glue or tape, *optional:* stapler and staples
- markers
- paper punch
- thin ribbon or string

Directions

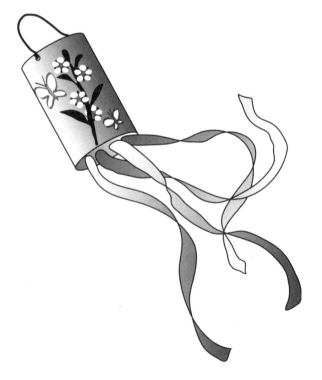

1. Draw spring designs on the colored paper with markers. Flowers, birds, and insects are good choices.

2. Overlap the long edges of the paper about $\frac{1}{2}''$, and then glue them together to form a tube.

3. Glue crepe paper streamers, tissue paper strips, or paper strips to the bottom of the tube (or use a stapler to fasten them), so they hang down to flutter in the wind.

4. Punch holes on either side of the tube at the top.

5. Thread the ribbon or string through the holes for hanging.

Fingerpaint Monoprints

In most kinds of printing, many copies are made from one original. In monoprinting, only one print is made. Fingerpainting is a fine way to create monoprints. The prints make great papers for binding handmade books, creating collages, crafting custom desk accessories, and wrapping special gifts.

Materials

- fingerpaint paper or plastic-coated freezer paper
- fingerpaint in several colors or powdered tempera mixed with laundry starch.
- copy paper or drawing paper
- old shirts to protect clothing, newspapers to protect table surfaces and the floor
- *optional:* various items for texture, such as combs, sponges, wadded plastic bags, wrinkled aluminum foil, and pieces of roughly woven cloth

Directions

1. Do a fingerpainting on the shiny side of the freezer paper.

2. Experiment with tools such as combs, sponges, wadded plastic bags, wrinkled aluminum foil, and pieces of roughly woven cloth to create textures.

3. Before the paint dries, press a sheet of copy paper onto the fingerpainting. Gently smooth it down.

4. Peel the papers apart.

5. If there is still paint on the freezer paper, do another print. If there is no paint left on the freezer paper, add more and do another fingerpainting.

6. Let the prints dry.

Extension: Create a monoprint by drawing on a recycled plexiglass box picture frame with water-soluble crayons (available at art supply stores). Wet a sheet of paper and lay it down on top of a towel. Put the drawing facedown on the wet paper. Press down. Peel the paper off the plastic.

Pencil Eraser Pointillism

Some post-Impressionist painters, including Georges Seurat, believed that colors could be mixed in the eye and mind of the viewer. They painted with dots of color placed close together. This method of painting is known as "pointillism." Create a pointillist painting of your own.

Materials

- egg carton lid (mixing tray)
- tempera in primary colors
- pencil with a round eraser on the end
- painting paper (not larger than 8″ x 10″)
- *optional:* reproductions of Seurat paintings from a book or online

Directions

1. In pencil, sketch a simple landscape with sky, hills, a lake, and trees.

2. Pour a puddle of each color of paint into the mixing tray.

3. Dip the eraser in a puddle of paint, and then stamp it onto the drawing, creating a dot. To make light blue for the sky, print white dots between the blue dots. To make green trees, print yellow dots between the blue dots. To make purple hills, print red dots between the blue dots.

4. Cover the entire surface of the painting with dots.

5. View your painting from a distance.

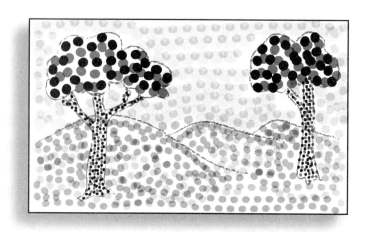

Alternate: Use paper-punch dots to make pointillist mosaics. Save the various colors of dots in separate resealable plastic sandwich bags or plastic margarine tubs.

Mother's Day: Magazine Beads

String these hand-crafted beads for a special Mother's Day gift.

Materials for each necklace

- glossy pages from magazines, catalogs, or junk mail
- scissors
- glue
- toothpick
- tapestry needle
- nylon thread or button and carpet thread

Directions

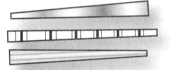

1. Choose a page with lots of color from magazines, catalogs, or junk mail.

2. Cut the page into very narrow strips.

3. Wrap each strip around the end of a toothpick. Make the first layer wide by bringing the strip around and overlapping it slightly.

4. As you continue to wrap, build thickness toward the center of the bead.

5. Fasten the end of the strip in place with a drop of white glue.

6. Slip the bead off the toothpick.

7. Repeat as many times as necessary to create enough beads for an 18″ necklace.

8. Using the needle and thread, string the beads.

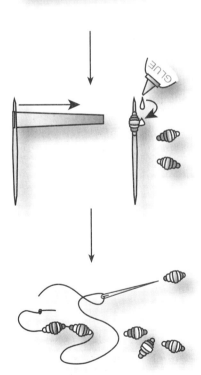

Optional: To make a more durable necklace, paint the finished magazine beads with clear acrylic medium.

Handmade beads may also be created from salt and flour clay or papier-mâché.

Quilt Blocks

Pioneers reused the cloth from flour sacks, sugar sacks, and worn-out clothing to create warm, attractive quilts for their beds. Design your own quilt square. Put the squares together to create a quilt wall.

Materials

- white paper
- pencil
- watercolor markers

Directions

1. Bring the short side of the white paper sheet up to meet the long side. Crease the resulting diagonal, and then cut off the extra flap, leaving a triangle.

2. Bring one point of the folded side of the triangle up to meet the opposite point and fold.

3. Unfold the paper. You will have two diagonal fold lines on a square.

4. Bring one side of the square up to meet the other side, creating a rectangle. Repeat in the opposite direction, forming a square.

5. Fold the folded square in half. Repeat in the opposite direction.

6. Unfold. The white paper square will have four identical squares with fold lines as shown.

7. Use the markers to color the sections of one of the four squares. You may leave some of the sections white.

8. Color the other three squares exactly the same way, or use mirror-image symmetry. (See symmetry project on page 51.)

Sample:

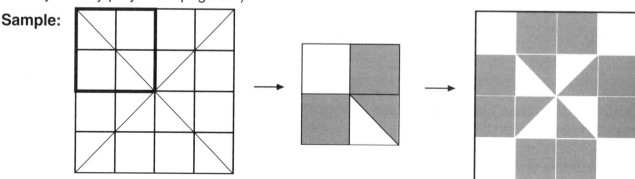

Anthropomorph-Animals

When fictional animals wear clothes and talk, they are not really animals; they are people. Making animals act like humans is called *anthropomorphism.** In this project, have fun creating animals that are really people in disguise.

Materials

- copy paper
- crayons or markers
- pencils
- magazines, books, or the Internet for reference

Directions

1. Find a picture of an animal in a book or magazine.

2. Draw the animal. Do not worry if your drawing does not look like the original. It is just a starting point.

3. Draw the animal again, only this time make it do something only humans can do, such as drive a car, read a book, or play baseball.

4. You may wish to find pictures of humans doing these activities to give you more visual information. Don't be afraid to add clothing, shoes, or hats. Four-footed creatures may stand on their hind legs. If you want a snake to hold something, you will have to get creative.

Optional: Look at children's picture books or books by cartoonists for ideas.

**anthro* means "man" and *morph* means "form."

Sunrise Scene: Watercolor Wash

Watercolor painters can create beautiful skies with a few brush strokes because they let the water do most of the work. This technique is called a wash. Use a watercolor wash to recreate a spring sunrise.

Materials for each painting

- paper for painting
- watercolor pans
- brush
- dark blue or purple construction paper
- water container

Directions

1. Moisten the paints with a few drops of water in each pan.

2. Paint the entire front surface of the paper with water.

3. While the paper is still very wet, dip the brush into blue paint.

4. Draw the wet brush quickly and smoothly across the top of the page.

5. Quickly dip the brush in water again. It will still have blue paint in it. That's fine. Draw it across the page just touching the bottom edge of the last stroke. It will be paler and it should blend. Repeat once more.

6. Dip the brush in the water, then in the orange paint. Draw it across the page just touching the lower edge of the last blue stroke. It should blend. Repeat.

7. Dip the brush in the water, then into the red paint. Draw the brush across the page. All of the colors will dry much lighter than they appear when wet.

8. Cut low hill shapes out of the blue or purple construction paper. Glue them along the bottom edge of the dried painting. You may wish to paint the hills on the paper. Make sure the wash is dry before you add the hills.

Dad's Car Service Record Pocket

Help your dad keep all of the service records for his car in one place with this handy pocket.

Materials for each pocket

- recycled mailing envelope 9" x 12" or larger with a working brass fastener
- sheet of colored construction paper
- markers
- glue
- gummed reinforcements

Directions

1. Glue construction paper to the side of the envelope with the address to cover up the label.

2. Draw car-related designs on the colored paper. These may be road signs such as "Stop," "Slow," "No Left Turn," or they may be pictures of vehicles. Feel free to decorate the page with collaged pictures from magazines instead of drawing them.

3. Put a gummed reinforcement on either side of the hole in the flap of the envelope.

4. Make a label by hand or on the computer that says "Service Records."

Alternate: Collage automobile pictures on the outside of a shoebox. Label the lid.

Note: Any container that closes securely and may be carried in the trunk of a car will work for storing receipts.

Hot Air Balloon Pictures

On June 5, 1783, the Montgolfier brothers, a pair of French papermakers, launched the first successful hot air balloon, and the age of flight was born. Around the world, enthusiasts still gather in early summer for balloon festivals. Capture the excitement with a tissue paper collage.

Materials for each balloon picture

- tissue paper in bright colors
- white paper
- brown construction paper
- starch, diluted white glue, or gloss acrylic medium
- paintbrush
- scissors
- brown thread

Directions

1. Cut several large balloon shapes out of tissue paper.

2. Arrange them on the white paper. Paint over each one with starch, glue, or acrylic medium. They may overlap.

3. Cut designs for the balloons out of other colors of tissue. Lay them on top of the original shapes and brush them in place.

4. Add a brown rectangle below each balloon for the passenger basket and four pieces of thread going down from each balloon to the basket.

Alternates:

1. Create "stained glass" balloons, similar to the "stained glass butterflies" on page 92, to display in classroom windows.

2. Create individual balloons from colored construction paper and magazine collage. Write the names of the artists on the baskets and display the balloons on a bulletin board covered with blue paper.

3. Use papier-mâché to cover sturdy party balloons. Paint the finished balloons and hang them from the ceiling. Use small product boxes, such as tea boxes, for the baskets, or fold boxes from brown construction paper.

Spatter Painting

Capture interesting natural shapes with a technique similar to airbrushing.

Materials for each painting

- variety of leaves
- tempera
- clean, recycled toothbrush
- small square of wire screen (for a screen door or window) with edges protected by masking tape
- paper for painting

Directions

1. Arrange several leaves on the paper. They should not overlap.

2. Dip the toothbrush in tempera.

3. Hold the screen above the paper. Rub the toothbrush across the screen, spattering the paper with dots of paint. Spatter enough paint to define the edges of all of the leaves. Let the paint dry.

4. Move the leaves. They may overlap parts of their previous locations. Clean the screen and repeat step three with a different color.

5. Repeat step four at least once more.

Extension:

1. Compare the results of this project with "Watercolor Glazes" on page 20. Notice the difference in texture.

2. Cut stencils out of copy paper. Use the same spatter technique. For the stencil, use either the piece that was cut out or the paper from which it was cut.

This Is My Neighborhood

Take pride in the landmarks that make your neighborhood unique. Draw or paint an interesting local building, mountain, or monument.

Materials for each artwork

- pencil and sketching paper
- photographs of local houses, buildings, or landmarks
- paper for painting
- tempera, crayons, markers, or watercolor paints
- paintbrushes
- water

Directions

1. Plan your painting by sketching the landmark. Use the photograph as reference.

2. Sketch the landmark on the painting paper.

3. Use tempera, crayons, markers, or watercolor paints to finish the painting.

Sources for photographs:

- Newspaper and junk mail pictures
- Photocopies of photographs taken by the teacher
- Photographs contributed by students

Alternatives:

1. Sit outside and draw the school building from different angles.

2. As homework, have each student draw the house across the street from theirs, and then use that sketch as the basis for an in-class painting.

Dyed Paper

Create some patriotic red, white, and blue patterns by folding and dyeing paper.

Materials for each piece of decorated paper

- white paper dinner napkins
- slightly diluted red and blue tempera, food coloring, or Easter egg dye in foam egg carton cups
- newspaper or tarp to protect table surface

Directions

1. The napkin is already folded. Do not unfold it. Fold it once more in each direction, diagonally. This creates a triangle.

2. Dip the center point of the folded triangle in red. Allow the napkin to absorb the paint. Dip each of the two end points in blue.

3. Open the napkin very carefully and lay it on a protected table surface to dry.

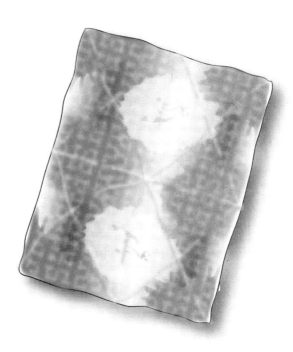

Optional: Fold the top of each dyed napkin over a piece of red or blue yarn. Tie the pieces of yarn together to create a string of pennants.

Extension: Experiment with different types of paper. Stiffer papers may need to be crinkled and soaked in water before dipping in color.

Travel Journal

Keep track of all your summer travels in a unique, handmade travel journal.

Materials for each journal

- masking tape
- 6–8 sheets of copy paper
- two 9″ x 12″ sheets of chipboard plus a 12″ x ½″ spine
- two 11″ x 18″ sheets of construction paper or decorative paper
- one 16″ x 23″ sheet of decorative self-adhesive vinyl shelf liner, colored bond paper, or wrapping paper.
- stapler and staples
- glue

Directions

1. Arrange the two sheets of chipboard on the shelf liner with the spine between them. Allow about ¼″ between the spine and each larger sheet. This is very important. The paper or vinyl between the sheets acts as a hinge. Without those two spaces, the book will not close.

2. Adhere the sheets to the shelf liner or bond. Younger students will need help. The self-adhesive vinyl wrinkles easily. You should have a 2″ margin all the way around. Fold the corners in first, then the top and bottom, then the sides. Put the finished cover aside.

3. Staple the 6–8 blank pages together. The staples should be close to the long edge and not more than ½″ apart. Think of this step as stitching with a stapler.

4. Position the edge of the stapled pages against the spine. Hold in place with three strips of masking tape in the front and three in the back: one at the top, one in the middle, and one at the bottom. Each strip should be about four inches long and should go across the edge of chipboard onto the book page.

5. Glue a sheet of construction paper to the inside front, covering the chipboard, the masking tape strips, and the first page of the book. Repeat with the other sheet of construction paper at the back of the book.

Alternates: Use one of the other binding techniques presented in this book. Use trimmed, recycled road maps instead of construction paper for the end papers.

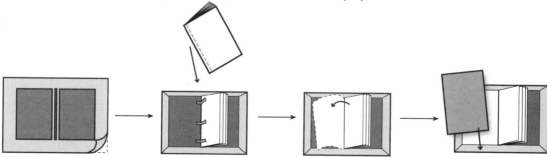

Design a Movie Poster

What would summer be without movies? Posters outside a theater help you decide which film to see. Design a poster that will convince your friends to see your favorite.

Materials for each poster

- copy paper
- markers, crayons, or construction paper
- scissors
- glue
- pencil
- eraser

Directions

1. In pencil, print the name of the movie and the star. The print should be large and clear. You may wish to use a bright color outlined in black for each letter. If so, allow space for the wider letters.

2. Draw a picture to show what the movie is about.

3. Color your poster.

Extensions:

1. Using a computer and scanner, copy all of the posters. Reduce them to thumbnails to fit all of them on one page. Print a copy for each member of the class.

2. Design a cover for your favorite music CD.

Windsong
☆☆☆☆☆
starring
Blaze
the
Wonder
Horse

His heroic rescue of the girl who loved him will touch your heart!

Journey to the Stars

Some science fiction illustrators use models to help them draw. They create their own model spacecraft from junk. Build a model spaceship, and then use it to paint a journey to the stars.

Materials for each spaceship

- cardboard tube or paper plates stapled together
- small pieces of recycled junk such as buttons or paper clips
- glue
- scissors
- tagboard or cardboard

Directions

1. If you are building a rocket, add a nose cone and fins to the tube.

   Hints: You can make a cone by cutting a slit from any point on the outside of a paper circle to the center. Shift the paper on either side of the slit to change the size and shape of the cone. Glue the overlapping edges in place.

   Adding fins to your rocket is easier if you cut slits in the bottom of the tube.

2. If you are creating a ship for deep space, it will probably have a saucer shape. It might even be a double saucer connected by tubes. Staple paper plates together, and then glue on small items.

3. Paint your ship or cover it with foil.

4. Use your model to create a drawing or painting of a ship in space. Include some individual stars and planets in the background, as well as galaxies and clouds of gas. Visit NASA's site online or the library for photographs of interesting objects in outer space.

Extension: Write a science fiction story. Use your model to help you draw the illustrations. Bind it into a book.

Ambivalent Profiles

Ambivalent means to have two equal values. Is this picture two faces or one vase?

Materials for each ambivalent profile picture

- copy paper
- pencil
- black construction paper
- sketching paper
- scissors
- glue

Directions

1. On one half of the sketching paper, draw the profile of a partner.

2. Do not include the entire head. Go back only as far as the front edge of the ears. The top of the head should be close to the top of the paper. The chin should hit the bottom of the paper.

3. Cut out the profile. Use it as a pattern to cut two copies from black construction paper

4. Match the flat side of one construction paper profile to the left edge of the white paper.

5. Turn the remaining construction paper profile over and match the flat edge to the right edge of the white paper. The two profiles should face each other.

6. Glue both profiles in place.

Alternates:

1. Use the profiles created in the "Silhouettes" activity on page 63.

2. Use black paint or black markers to fill in the silhouettes instead of construction paper.

3. Draw the profile from a single original digital photograph reproduced for the group.

Red and Blue Tiling

Make a patriotic design using red, white, and blue tiling.

Materials for each tiling

- white paper
- blue and red markers
- tile pattern from below
- scissors

Directions

1. Cut out the tile pattern.

2. Match the top edge of the pattern to the top edge of your paper.

3. Trace around the pattern. Match the edges of the pattern to the lines you just drew and trace the pattern again. Repeat to cover the page.

4. Color the design with red and blue markers. If desired, use the white of the page for a third color.

Extension: On a sheet of $\frac{1}{4}''$ graph paper, design a tiling. Color it with colored pencils. Create a pattern like the one below so others can recreate your design.

Tile Pattern:

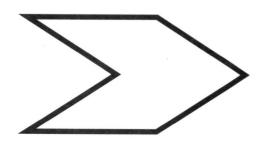

Sample of Tiling:

Crayon Fireworks

Celebrate the 4th of July or any special occasion with this fireworks picture.

Materials for each fireworks picture

- paper
- crayons

Directions

1. Make dots at random on the paper.

2. With the dot as the center, draw short, radiating crayon lines. Press hard to make the colors intense and keep the lines close together.

3. Draw another group of radiating lines outside the first.

4. Repeat the process. Make each dot the center of two to four radiating circles of color.

Variations:

1. Leave some space between the color bursts. Paint over the drawing with black tempera, watercolor, or ink to create a resist effect.

2. Color over the entire finished drawing with black crayon. Scratch parallel lines in the top layer revealing the fireworks underneath.

3. Color random color patterns in crayon all over the page. Color over with black crayon. Use a paper clip to scratch out a fireworks display.

Expanded Paper Twirlers

Hang these twirlers on your porch to catch the summer breeze.

Materials for each twirler

- red, white, or blue construction paper
- scissors
- string or paper gift ribbon for hanging

Directions

1. Use a large can or lid to draw a circle in the paper.

2. Cut out the circle.

3. Starting at the edge of the circle, cut a spiral toward the center as shown below.

4. Use a pencil to poke a hole for the string in the center of the spiral.

5. Attach the string and pull gently down on the outer edge of the spiral, if necessary. It should fall into a spring shape.

Alternate: Cut spirals from squares, triangles, or other geometric shapes.

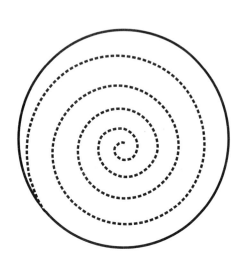

A Pressed Flower Bookmark

Create this beautiful floral bookmark for yourself or as a gift for someone special.

Materials for each bookmark

- several small, flat-faced flowers, such as violas or pansies
- waxed paper
- heavy books that will not be needed for at least a week
- strips of cover stock or tagboard
- clear, self-adhesive shelf paper
- white glue

For best results, do the first step of this project before a long weekend or vacation.

Directions

1. Put a piece of waxed paper on the table, put the flower, face-up, on top of it. Put another sheet of waxed paper on top. Put some heavy books on top. Leave them in place for a week.

2. Carefully transfer the flowers from the waxed paper to the tagboard strip. Glue them in place and let the glue dry.

3. With the backing still on, cut the self-adhesive shelf paper to match the cardboard.

4. Peel off the backing and cover the front of the bookmark.

Alternate: Cover each flower with clear tape.

Sun or Moon Shields

Native Americans who lived on the plains made shields from stretched buffalo hide. They decorated the shields with symbols of courage and power. Create your own shield with a symbol for the sun or the moon.

Materials for each shield

- brown paper grocery sack flattened out
- tempera in egg carton cups
- paintbrush
- pencil

Directions

1. Crinkle up the paper from the sack, then wet it and stain it with black and red watercolor. (See "Wet-on-Wet Book Covers" on page 6.) Let the paint dry. Cut the paper into a large circle or oval.

2. Sketch a symbol for the sun or moon onto the textured paper. Add facial features, designs, or rays. Your symbol should fill the center of the shield. Draw geometric designs to create a border.

3. Paint the symbol and border with tempera.

Ladybug Refrigerator Door Magnets

Even people who hate insects love ladybugs. They don't sting, they are pretty, and they eat aphids. Make a ladybug magnet to hold notes onto the refrigerator door.

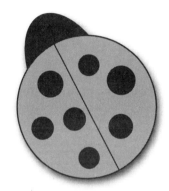

Materials for each magnet

- small sheets of red and black construction paper
- scissors
- glue
- purchased magnet strip
- black watercolor marker

Directions

1. Cut an oval shape from the black paper.

2. Cut a smaller red circle from the red paper.

3. Glue the red circle on top of one end of the oval.

4. Draw a line down the middle of the red paper to separate the wings. Add dots.

5. Attach a magnet strip to the underside of the ladybug.

Alternate: Look up other interesting beetles in the encyclopedia or online. Create a set of beetle magnets.

Pop Art

One purpose of art is to help people notice things they usually take for granted. Andy Warhol and other Pop artists painted pictures and created sculptures based on items we see every day. Subjects of Pop paintings include soup cans and cereal boxes. The paintings often use symmetry and repetition.

Materials

- empty product boxes, cans, plastic bottles, or jars
- paper for painting
- tempera
- paintbrushes
- pencils and rulers

Directions

1. Divide the paper into four equal sections.

2. Draw the same product box or can in each section.

3. Paint the box or can realistically in one section. In the next section, use complementary colors (across from each other on the color wheel). In the third section use tints, (pure colors plus white). In the last section, use tones (pure colors plus black).

Alternate: Paint all four sections the same way or have two paint schemes and create an alternating pattern.

Sailboat Aluminum Foil Plaque

This sailboat plaque is sure to be a hit for anyone who loves sailing!

Materials for each plaque

- corrugated cardboard
- heavy string or rug yarn
- glue
- aluminum foil
- tempera mixed with a few drops of liquid detergent

Directions

1. Draw a sailboat on the cardboard. Make your drawing large and simple.

2. Glue the heavy string or yarn down on the pencil lines to create a raised design.

3. Cover the front of the plaque with aluminum foil, dull side up. Gently press the foil down around the string or yarn. Use a pencil eraser to press down small areas. Fold extra foil to the back of the plaque and glue in place.

4. Paint the sea, the sky, the boat, and the sail with tempera.

Extension: Students may use this technique to create other pictures, such as the irises shown on the cover.

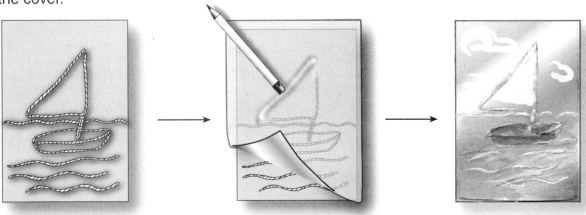

Autograph Book

International Friendship Day is August 4. Remember school and summer friends by having them sign this autograph book. Check the poetry section of the library for funny verses to use when it's your turn to sign.

Materials for each autograph book

- tagboard, cover stock, or index stock cut in half to $4\frac{1}{4}''$ x 11"
- stapler and staples, or needle and white button or carpet thread
- four or five sheets of copy paper, cut in half to $4\frac{1}{4}''$ x 11"
  optional: each page may be a different pastel color
- markers, collage materials, or colored pencils

Directions

1. Fold the cover and pages in half.

2. Staple or hand stitch on the fold.

3. Decorate the cover with markers, collage, or colored pencils.

4. Fold every other page up on the diagonal to keep messages private.

Alternate: Create an accordion autograph book. (See "Kwanzaa Accordion Book" on page 86.)

Where to Find More Ideas

Libraries and the Internet are brimming with art and craft ideas. Here are just a few of the hundreds of books and websites available.

Books:

Cusick, Dawn. *Paper & Fabric Mâché: 100 Imaginative & Ingenious Projects to Make.* Lark Books; Reprint Edition, 1995.

Golden, Alisa. *Creating Handmade Books.* Sterling Publications, 2000.

Kallevig, Christine Petrell. *Holiday Folding Stories: Storytelling and Origami Together for Holiday Fun.* Storytime Ink International, 1992.

Kohl, MaryAnn F. *Mudworks: Creative Clay, Dough, and Modeling Experiences.* Bright Ring Publishing, 1992.

Lawrence, Catherine. *Creative Crafting with Recycled Greeting Cards.* Sterling Publications; Cards edition, 1998.

Leland, Nina and Virginia Lee Williams. *Creative Collage Techniques.* North Light Books, 1994.

Maurer-Mathison, Diane V. with Jennifer Philippoff. *Paper Art: The Complete Guide to Papercraft Techniques.* Watson-Guptill Publications, 1997.

Stokes, Donald W. and Lillian and Ernest Williams. *The Butterfly Book: An Easy Guide to Butterfly Gardening, Identification, and Behavior.* Little, Brown, 1991

Welch, Nancy. *Creative Paper Art: Techniques for Transforming the Surface.* Sterling Publications, 2000.

Where to Find More Ideas (cont.)

Websites:

"Art Room Activities: Color Theory"
> http://members.cox.net/mrsparker2/activities.htm

"Craft Recipes for Year-Round Fun"
> http://www.geocities.com/holidayzone/recipes/dough.html

"Encyclopedia of Days"
> http://www.shagtown.com/days/

"Geometry: Online Interactive"
> http://www.scienceu.com/library/makeindex.cgi?SU_Subject=geometry&SU_Doctype=
> simulations

"How to Cut a Five-Pointed Star in One Snip"
> http://www.ushistory.org/betsy/flagstar.html

"The Idea Box"
> http://www.theideabox.com/

"Make-Stuff.com Crafts and Gifts Projects"
> http://www.make-stuff.com/projects/index.html

"Try Our Super Craft Projects" Kansas City, Kansas, Public Library
> http://www.kckpl.lib.ks.us/ys/crafts/Crafts.htm